EASY BAKE OVEN COOKBOOK

Easy and Amazing Baking Recipes for Young Chefs

Hazel Cornett

Table of Contents

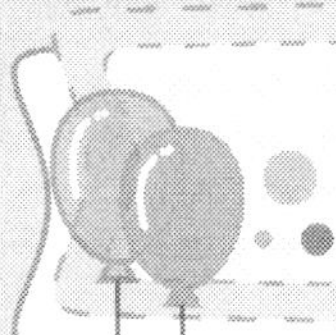

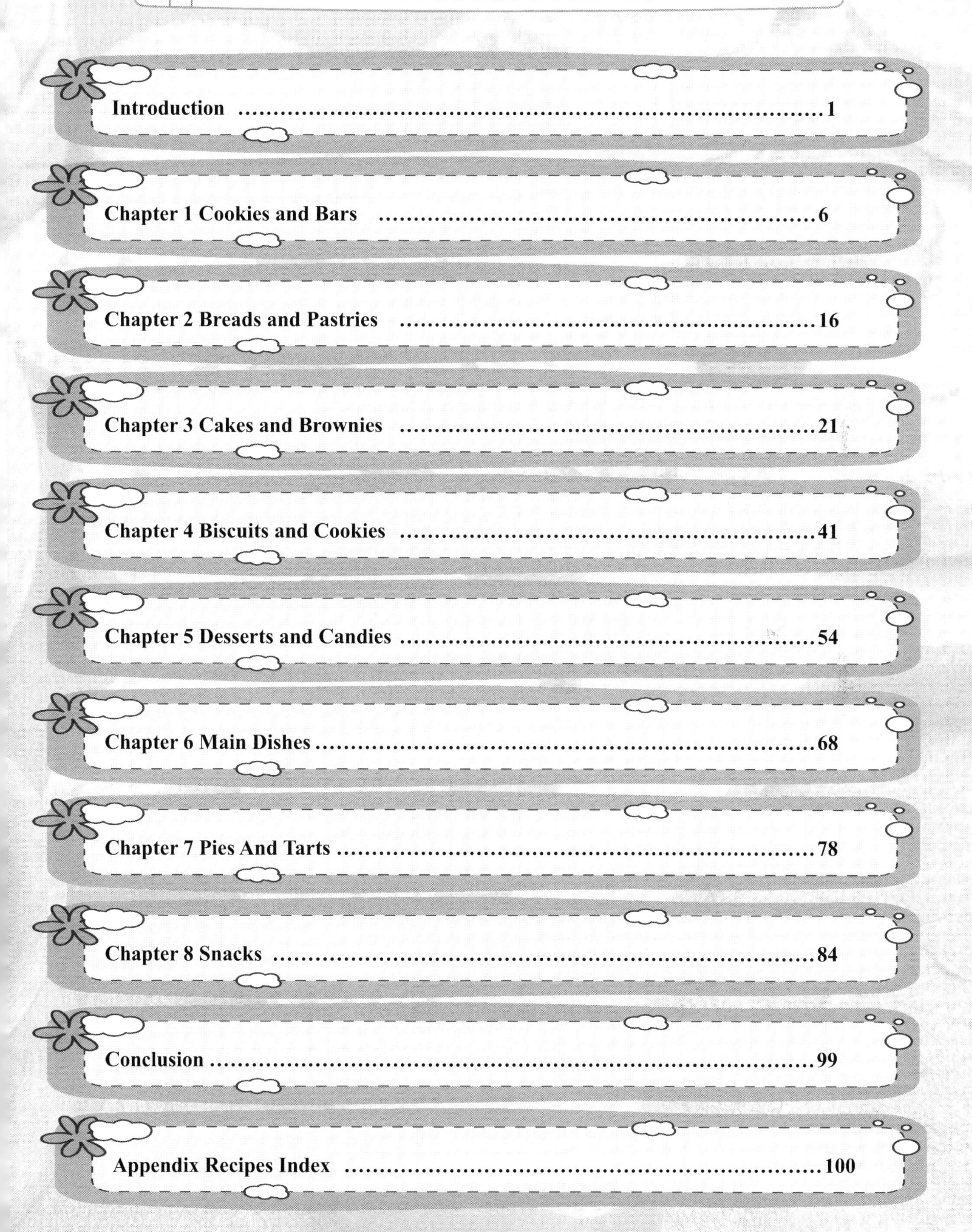

Introduction

The Easy-Bake Oven was a toy oven introduced in 1963. It's still being manufactured today as a baking tool for kids. The older versions of the oven used an ordinary light bulb as a heat source. However, new models use a heating element like those used in ordinary ovens.

Of all the fantastical and technologically-advanced gadgets toymakers have invented over the centuries, only a few really capture children's imaginations. And the Easy-Bake Oven is one of those toys. It's not the fanciest and most expensive toys that mean the most to kids; it's when their dreams become realized. The Easy-Bake Oven does this for both girls and boys who dream of creating delicious food in a real functioning oven.

The Easy-Bake Oven has stamped itself onto the minds of children all around the world. It's not a passing fashion or fad; for over 40 years, it's been an obsession for kids. Through all its different incarnations, styles, and colors, the oven has endured as the go-to toy for kids who want to explore the world of baking.

Kids love whisking the ingredients of the simple recipes together, plopping them into a pan, and then taking out the cooked results a few minutes later. These little chefs even enjoy eating their yummy creations, despite many adults doubting the true edibility of these goodies!

For kids, the oven is a charming and empowering tool. Not only can they cook just like their elders, but they're satisfied with the tangible, edible fruits of their labor. And although the oven is mainly for baking goods such as cupcakes or cookies, it makes all sorts of other treats, too, including pizza, candy, peanut brittle, and fudge.

To create cooked delights, children slide a loaded baking pan through a slot and into the heating chamber. Then, they can look closely through a tiny window at the ingredients being baked right before their eyes. After a few minutes, the cooked creation is pushed through to the cooling chamber. After it's left to cool for 5 minutes, kids can then indulge in their freshly-created treat—or share it with friends or loved ones. It doesn't take any special baking skill or knowledge to make the Easy-Bake Oven respond to your culinary requests.

Now, the question arises: at what age is the Easy-Bake Oven safe for kids to use. After all, it involves electricity and a heating element and can therefore be a hazardous item near children. The manufacturers recommend that it's not used by kids under the age of eight years. It's the perfect, unique gift for slightly older children with the curiosity and enthusiasm to learn more about baking.

Note for Parents and Guardians

The Easy-Bake Oven is a piece of electrical equipment. It requires some simple steps to be followed by parents/guardians for its safe use.

Parents/guardians should help children hand wash all the pans and utensils before using the Easy-Bake Oven for the first time. All equipment should then be thoroughly cleaned by hand after every use.

Children should always be helped/supervised when using the pan tool to move the baking pan into the cooking and cooling chambers. Children should be advised that the pan will become very hot and may harm them if not handled correctly.

Make sure the oven, tools, and pans are completely cool before handling.

Unplug the oven whenever it's not in use.

Read the user manual before use.

Never leave empty pans in the oven.

Never plug the oven in near water or wet surfaces.

Make sure children never put their fingers in the hot oven.

Parents/guardians should examine the oven periodically for potential hazards, and any damaged parts should be repaired or replaced.

Tips for Kids

The new oven will smell because of the oil used to protect its metal parts. When the oven is heated up, you'll see some smoke or vapors. Don't worry; this is non-toxic and will disappear quickly.

As the oven and food will get very hot, never handle them bare-handed. Always use cooking gloves—just like a professional chef.

When baking, the oven interior, top and back will be very hot. So don't touch.

To prevent electric shock, don't put the oven in water or use it anywhere near water.

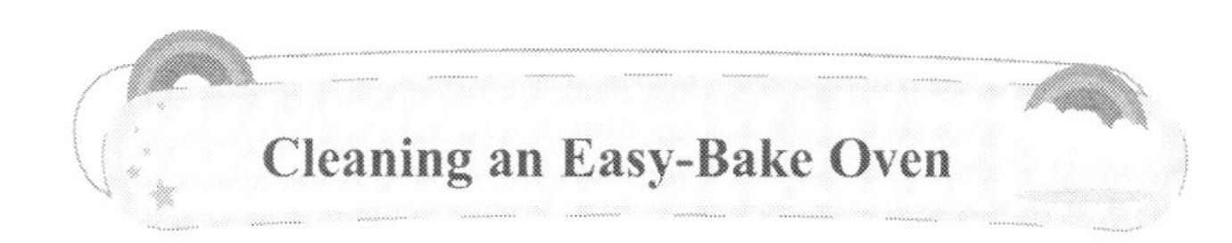

Cleaning an Easy-Bake Oven

Although Easy-Bake Ovens are a small children's toy, they bake real desserts and snacks. Just like a regular oven or other kitchen appliances, you'll need to every so often clean your Easy-Bake Oven, including inside the baking chamber.

Turn off the Easy-Bake Oven's power and unplug it before you clean it. The oven mustn't be on

or near any electrical source. Allow it to cool down completely before cleaning it.

Children mustn't clean the Easy-Bake Oven by themselves. An adult must help or supervise them.

Never plug in the oven around or near water.

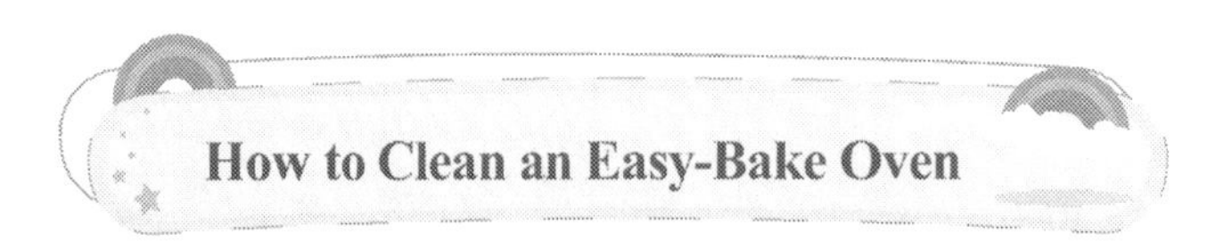

How to Clean an Easy-Bake Oven

Put the oven on a towel when cleaning it.

Don't forget to clean all parts of the oven and its utensils, including the baking pan and pan tool.

You won't need to take the oven apart for cleaning. Most pieces of the oven are not to be removed.

Try covering the baking pan with foil when baking to reduce build-up.

Easy-Bake Ovens can be cleaned using a washcloth, paper towels, or other rags.

You'll need a long, thin tool to reach inside the baking compartment to knock off crusted-on food.

Use a dab of dish soap to clean the oven. You can easily clean an Easy Bake Oven with a little water and soap.

Take some dish soap, and mix it with glass cleaner. Then dab this mixture onto your washcloth or paper towel.

Wipe the inside and outside of the oven. Repeat this several times.

You can also lightly spray the oven with a diluted mixture of detergent. Be sure to wipe well.

You can also use white vinegar to clean the oven if you prefer a chemical-free option. Mix white vinegar with equal parts water.

Another chemical-free option is to use lemon juice for cleaning. Lemon juice will also help make the oven smell good and, if you add a bit of liquid soap to the lemon juice, it will help remove stains.

Thoroughly dry the Easy-Bake Oven once you've wiped it down with your cleaning mixture of choice.

Wipe the oven with a dry towel to remove any moisture or liquid. You could also use paper towels.

Remember to dry both the outside and the inside of the Easy-Bake Oven. If you live in a warm climate, you can let the oven sit outside for a while to completely dry.

Now, let's get started using your Easy-Bake Oven to create some delicious, yummy food!

Chapter 1 Cookies and Bars

Choco Peanut Butter Bars

Prep time: 10 minutes | Cook Time: 5 minutes | Serves: 6

Ingredients:

Anti-sticking baking spray
6 graham crackers
6 tablespoons peanut butter
6 tablespoons mini chocolate chips

Preparation:

1. Plug in the easy bake oven, preheating it for 15 minutes. 2. On a Graham cracker, apply a thin layer of peanut butter. 3. Sprinkle chocolate chips on top. 4. Lay out the bars onto the baking pan about 1½-inch apart. 5. Bake in the preheated oven for 5 minutes. 6. After cooking time is finished, with pan pusher, shove the baking pan into the "Cooling Chamber". 7. Give it about five minutes to cool down. 8. Carefully turn the chocolate peanut butter bars onto a platter to serve and enjoy.

Per Serving: Calories 233; Fat 12.5g; Sodium 238mg; Carbs 26.9g; Fiber 1.3g; Sugar 11.9g; Protein 5g

Corn Strawberry Bars

Prep time: 15 minutes | Cook Time: 18 minutes | Serves: 3

Ingredients:

Anti-sticking baking spray
1 tablespoon cornflakes, crushed
3 tablespoons flour
1 tablespoon butter, softened
2 teaspoons strawberry jam
1 teaspoon sugar

Preparation:

1. Plug in the easy bake oven, preheating it for 15 minutes. 2. Put flour, cornflakes, butter, and sugar in a bowl and whisk to incorporate coarsely. 3. Reserve 2 tablespoons of mixture and set aside. 4. Lay out residual mixture into the baking pan. 5. Layer the strawberry jam on it. 6. Trickle the reserved mixture over strawberry jam and gently press down. 7. Bake in the preheated oven for 18 minutes. 8. After cooking time is finished, with pan pusher, shove the baking pan into the "Cooling Chamber". 9. Give it about five minutes to cool down. 10. Cut into bars with a sharp knife. Then carefully turn the strawberry bars onto a platter to serve and enjoy.

Per Serving: Calories 86; Fat 3.9g; Sodium 32mg; Carbs 11.9g; Fiber 0.2g; Sugar 1.4g; Protein 0.9g

Butter Cookies

Prep time: 15 minutes | Cook Time: 5 minutes | Serves: 12

Ingredients:

3 teaspoons brown sugar
6 teaspoons butter
¼ cup flour
1 pinch salt
⅛ teaspoon cream of tartar
2 pinches baking soda
Anti-sticking baking spray
3 teaspoons sugar

Preparation:

1. Plug in the easy bake oven, preheating it for 10 minutes. 2. Spritz baking spray on the baking pan, followed by dusting with flour. 3. In a bowl, merge flour with all ingredients until a dough forms. Cut the dough into small equal portions. 4. Portion the cookie dough onto the baking pan about 1½-inch apart. 5. Bake in the preheated oven for 5 minutes. 6. After cooking time is finished, with pan pusher, shove the baking pan into the "Cooling Chamber". 7. Give it about five minutes to cool down. 8. Carefully turn the cookies onto a platter to serve and enjoy.
Per Serving: Calories 33; Fat 1.9g; Sodium 39mg; Carbs 3.7g; Fiber 0.1g; Sugar 1.7g; Protein 0.3g

Delicious Blueberry Danish

Prep time: 15 minutes | Cook Time: 12 minutes | Serves: 8

Ingredients:

¼ cup biscuit mix
½ tablespoon margarine
Anti-sticking baking spray
4 teaspoons milk
¾ teaspoon sugar
½ tablespoon pie filling, blueberry

Preparation:

1. Plug in the easy bake oven, preheating it for 15 minutes. 2. Spritz baking spray on the baking pan, followed by dusting with flour. 3. Merge biscuit mix with margarine and sugar in a bowl and whisk to incorporate into a dough. 4. Divide the dough into small-sized balls. 5. Lay out half of dough balls onto the baking pan about 1½-inch apart. 6. Create an indentation in the center by gently pressing your thumb. 7. Then, fill the indentation with blueberry pie filling. 8. Bake in the preheated oven for 12 minutes. 9. After cooking time is finished, with pan pusher, shove the baking pan into the "Cooling Chamber". 10. Give it about five minutes to cool down. 11. Carefully turn the delicious Danish onto a platter to serve and enjoy.
Per Serving: Calories 26; Fat 1.3g; Sodium 55mg; Carbs 3.1g; Fiber 0.1g; Sugar 1.2g; Protein 0.4g

Raisin Scones

Prep time: 15 minutes | Cook Time: 15 minutes | Serves: 6

Ingredients:

⅛ teaspoon baking powder
1 tablespoon raisins
⅓ cup flour, all-purpose
1 tablespoon sugar
⅛ teaspoon salt
Anti-sticking baking spray
⅛ teaspoon baking soda
1 tablespoon sour cream
⅛ teaspoon cream of tartar
1 tablespoon butter

Preparation:

1. Plug in the easy bake oven, preheating it for 15 minutes. 2. Spritz baking spray on the baking pan, followed by dusting with flour. 3. In a small bowl, merge sour cream with baking soda, keeping it aside. 4. In a separate bowl, mingle flour with remaining ingredients. 5. Till it resembles coarse crumbs, incorporate butter into the dry ingredients. 6. Fold in the sour cream mixture until the mixture is moistened. 7. Finally, incorporate the raisins into the mixture. 8. Briefly knead the dough. 9. Pat the dough into ball that is approximately ½ inch thick. 10. Cut the dough into wedges, and then arrange the wedges onto the baking pan. 11. Bake in the preheated oven for 15 minutes. 12. After cooking time is finished, with pan pusher, shove the baking pan into the "Cooling Chamber". 13. Give it about five minutes to cool down. 14. Carefully turn the scones onto a platter to serve and enjoy.

Per Serving: Calories 59; Fat 2.4g; Sodium 93mg; Carbs 8.7g; Fiber 0.3g; Sugar 2.9g; Protein 0.9g

Flavorful Cherry Danish

Prep time: 15 minutes | Cook Time: 12 minutes | Serves: 8

Ingredients:

¾ teaspoon sugar
4 teaspoons milk
Anti-sticking baking spray
¼ cup biscuit mix
½ tablespoon margarine
½ tablespoon cherry pie filling

Preparation:

1. Plug in the easy bake oven, preheating it for 15 minutes. 2. Spritz baking spray on the baking pan, followed by dusting with flour. 3. Put biscuit mix, margarine, milk and sugar into medium-sized bowl and whisk to incorporate into a dough. 4. Divide the dough into small-sized balls. 5. Lay out the dough balls onto the baking pan about 1½-inch apart. 6. Create an indentation in the center by gently pressing your thumb. 7. Then, fill the indentation with cherry pie filling. 8. Bake in the preheated oven for 12 minutes. 9. After cooking time is finished, with pan pusher, shove the baking pan into the "Cooling Chamber". 10. Give it about five minutes to cool down. 11. Carefully turn the Cherry Danish onto a platter to serve and enjoy.

Per Serving: Calories 25; Fat 1.3g; Sodium 55mg; Carbs 3g; Fiber 0.1g; Sugar 0.9g; Protein 0.4g

Granola Bars

Prep time: 15 minutes | Cook Time: 10 minutes | Serves: 6

Ingredients:

¼ cup rolled oats
2 teaspoons butter, softened
1 teaspoon raisins
⅛ teaspoon vanilla extract
1 teaspoon mini chocolate chips, semisweet
3 teaspoons flour, all-purpose
Anti-sticking baking spray
⅛ teaspoon baking soda
1 teaspoon brown sugar, packed
1 teaspoon honey

Preparation:

1. Plug in the easy bake oven, preheating it for 15 minutes. 2. Spritz baking spray on the baking pan, followed by dusting with flour. 3. In a medium-sized bowl, merge together all ingredients until the mixture is well combined. 4. Portion the mixture onto the baking pan and gently press. 5. Bake in the preheated oven for 10 minutes. 6. After cooking time is finished, with pan pusher, shove the baking pan into the "Cooling Chamber". 7. Give it about five minutes to cool down. 8. Cut into bars with a sharp knife. Then carefully turn the granola bars onto a platter to serve and enjoy.

Per Serving: Calories 38; Fat 1.6g; Sodium 37mg; Carbs 5.4g; Fiber 0.4g; Sugar 2g; Protein 0.6g

Homemade White Chocolate Cookies

Prep time: 15 minutes | Cook Time: 12 minutes | Serves: 24

Ingredients:

¼ teaspoon baking powder
2 tablespoons brown sugar, firmly packed
2 tablespoons sugar
¼ teaspoon vanilla extract
4 teaspoons margarine
6 tablespoons flour, all-purpose
Anti-sticking baking spray
4 tablespoons white chocolate chips
2 teaspoons water

Preparation:

1. Plug in the easy bake oven, preheating it for 15 minutes. 2. Spritz baking spray on the baking pan, followed by dusting with flour. 3. Put sugars and margarine into medium-sized bowl and whisk to incorporate. 4. Put flour, baking powder, vanilla extract and water and whisk to incorporate thoroughly. 5. Gently blend in chocolate chips. 6. Split the dough into 24 balls and flatten them. 7. Bake in the preheated oven for 10-12 minutes. 8. Cook the remnant cookies in the same way. 9. Shift the baking pan on a countertop to cool down for approximately five minutes. 10. Carefully turn the cookies onto a platter to serve and enjoy.

Per Serving: Calories 26; Fat 1g; Sodium 9mg; Carbs 4g; Fiber 0.1g; Sugar 2.5g; Protein 0.3g

Chocolate Peanut Butter Bars

Prep time: 5 minutes | Cook Time: 5 minutes | Serves: 2

Ingredients:

2 tablespoons peanut butter
4 graham crackers
1 tablespoon Mini chocolate chips

Preparation:

1. Spread a thin layer of peanut butter on a graham cracker. 2. Top with mini chocolate chips. 3. Bake in the Easy-Bake Oven for 5 minutes. 4. Remove and spread the softened chocolate over the cracker. Allow the bar to cool slightly before eating.

Serving Suggestion: Serve with cold milk.

Variation Tip: You can use crushed walnuts for extra taste.

Per Serving: Calories 215.3; Carbohydrates 19.4g; Protein 3.7g; Fat 14.7g; Sodium 83.8mg; Fiber 1.1g

Little Prince Bars (With Dulce de Leche)

Prep time: 10 minutes (plus 2 hours for chilling) | Cook Time: 12 minutes | Serves: 2

Ingredients:

½ cup unsalted butter
4 tablespoons water
Pinch of salt
Dulce de leche, for serving
½ cup white sugar
1 teaspoon baking powder
1 cup plain all-purpose flour

Preparation:

1. Put the butter, salt, water, and sugar in a saucepan over low heat. Bring the mixture to a boil. 2. Remove the saucepan from the heat. Mix well. 3. Once the mixture is cool, add the flour and baking powder. Mix well. 4. Form the mixture into a ball. Place it in the refrigerator for 2 hours. 5. Roll the dough out between sheets of parchment paper. 6. Cut the dough into equal-sized squares. 7. Place the squares onto the prepared baking pan. You'll need to cook in batches. 8. Bake for about 12 minutes. 9. Let them cool completely on a wire rack before serving.

Serving Suggestion: Apply a good amount of dulce de leche to the top of one square. Place another square on top. Repeat until all the squares are used up.

Variation Tip: You can use another type of filling if you prefer.

Per Serving: Calories 1041; Fat 46.6g; Sodium 420mg; Carbs 153g; Fiber 1.9g; Sugar 50.g; Protein 2.2g

Orange Marmalade Bars

Prep time: 10 minutes | Cook Time: 21 minutes | Serves: 2

Ingredients:

1 tablespoon butter, softened
4 teaspoons sugar
1/3 cup flour
4 tablespoons almond milk
1/6 teaspoon baking soda
2 tablespoons quick-cook rolled oats
Dash of salt
5 teaspoons orange marmalade

Preparation:

1. Mix the sugar and butter along with the salt in a bowl until creamy. 2. Add the baking soda, flour, milk, and oats. Mix well. 3. Divide the batter into two prepared baking pans. 4. Press down a little on the mixture. 5. Spread the orange marmalade on the top of each. 6. Bake each for 21 minutes. 7. Once done, let the bars cool completely and then cut into small slices. 8. Serve and enjoy!

Serving Suggestion: Serve as a snack.
Variation Tip: Use coconut milk instead of almond milk
Per Serving: Calories 269; Fat 13.3g; Sodium 236mg; Carbs 36.6g; Fiber 1.6g; Sugar 16.9g; Protein 3.9g

Chocolate Coconut Bars

Prep time: 10 minutes | Cook Time: 10 minutes | Serves: 2

Ingredients:

¼ cup rolled oats
6 tablespoons coconut flour
1/8 teaspoon baking soda
1/8 teaspoon vanilla extract
2 teaspoons margarine, softened
1 teaspoon white sugar
1 teaspoon brown sugar
1 teaspoon semi-sweet mini chocolate chips
2 teaspoons coconut flakes

Preparation:

1. Mix the rolled oats, coconut flour, baking soda, vanilla extract, margarine, brown sugar, and white sugar in a bowl. 2. Fold in the chocolate chips and coconut flakes. Combine. 3. Press the mixture into the prepared baking pan. 4. Bake for 8 minutes. 5. Let the bar cool for 10 minutes before cutting it into squares. 6. Enjoy!

Serving Suggestion: Serve with milk.
Variation Tip: None, these bars are yummy just as they are!
Per Serving: Calories 297; Fat 12.6g; Sodium 221mg; Carbs 37g; Fiber 16.3g; Sugar 8.9g; Protein 8g

Strawberry Bars

Prep time: 20 minutes | Cook Time: 18 minutes | Serves: 1

Ingredients:

3 tablespoons flour
1 tablespoon cornflakes, crushed
1 tablespoon butter or margarine, softened
1 teaspoon sugar
2 teaspoons strawberry jam

Preparation:

1. Mix together the flour, cereal, butter, and sugar until crumbly. 2. Reserve 2 tablespoons of the mixture and set it aside. 3. Press the remaining mixture firmly into the Easy-Bake Oven baking pan. Spread with the jam. 4. Sprinkle the reserved mixture over the jam, pressing down gently. 5. Bake in the Easy-Bake Oven for 18 minutes.

Serving Suggestion: Serve it with a hot cup of coffee or even a cold glass of milk.

Variation Tip: Use brown sugar.

Per Serving: Calories 123.4; Fat 3.9g; Sodium 90.6mg; Carbohydrates 21.7g; Fiber 0.6g; Sugars 13.5g; Protein 1.7g

Six Layer Bars

Prep time: 10 minutes | Cook Time: 20 minutes | Serves: 3

Ingredients:

2 tablespoons margarine
1⁄3 cup graham cracker crumbs
2 tablespoons semi-sweet chocolate chips
3 tablespoons butterscotch chips
4 tablespoons coconut flakes
2 tablespoons condensed milk
1 tablespoon chopped walnuts

Preparation:

1. Melt the margarine in the microwave. Place it into the baking pan. 2. Spread the graham cracker crumbs evenly over the melted margarine. 3. Add a layer of chocolate chips and then a layer of butterscotch chips. 4. Add a layer of flaked coconut and walnuts. 5. Pour the condensed milk over the top. 6. Bake for 15–20 minutes. 7. Allow the bar to cool completely before cutting into pieces and serving.

Serving Suggestion: Serve with milk.

Variation Tip: Any other nuts can be used instead of walnuts.

Per Serving: Calories 317; Fat 20.8g; Sodium 226mg; Carbs 3.6g; Fiber 2.4g; Sugar 21.7g; Protein 3.2g

Apple Bar

Prep time: 5 minutes | Cook Time: 18 minutes | Serves: 2

Ingredients:

3 tablespoons flour
1 tablespoon crushed cornflakes
1 tablespoon soft butter or margarine
1 teaspoon sugar
2 teaspoons apple jelly
⅛ teaspoon ground cinnamon

Preparation:

1. In a bowl, mix the flour, cinnamon, cereal, butter, and sugar until crumbly. 2. Reserve 2 tablespoons of the crumbly mixture. Press the remaining mixture firmly into the baking pan. Spread with the jelly. 3. Sprinkle the reserved crumbly mixture over the jelly; press gently with your fingers. 4. Bake in the Easy-Bake Oven for 18 minutes. Allow the bar to cool before serving.

Serving Suggestion: Cut the bar into wedges before serving.

Variation Tip: Add some chopped nuts for crunch.

Per Serving: Calories 248; Carbohydrates 40.7g; Protein 2.5g; Fat 10.8g; Sodium 120.4mg; Fiber 0.7g

Oatmeal Fruit Bars

Prep time: 5 minutes | Cook Time: 21 minutes | Serves: 2

Ingredients:

1 tablespoon shortening or soft butter
6 teaspoons brown sugar
Dash of salt
¼ cup flour
3 tablespoons milk
⅛ teaspoon baking soda
2 tablespoons quick-cooking rolled oats
2 teaspoons apple sauce or marmalade

Preparation:

1. Mix the shortening, sugar, and salt in a bowl until creamed. 2. Add the flour, baking soda, oats, and milk. Mix well until it forms a soft dough. 3. Place half of the mixture into the greased baking pan. Press it down in the pan with your fingertips or the back of a spoon. 4. Spread with 2 teaspoons of apple sauce or marmalade. 5. Bake in the Easy-Bake Oven for about 21 minutes. 6. Let cool and cut into slices.

Serving Suggestion: Serve with milk.

Variation Tip: You can use dried fruit chunks for a chewier texture.

Per Serving: Calories 199.8; Carbohydrates 25.6g; Protein 3.6g; Fat 2.2g; Sodium 147.6mg; Fiber 4.8g

Prep time: 5 minutes | Cook Time: 18 minutes | Serves: 2

Ingredients:

3 tablespoons flour
1 tablespoon cornflakes, crushed
1 tablespoon butter or margarine, softened
1 teaspoon sugar
2 teaspoons raspberry jam

Preparation:

1. Mix together the flour, cornflakes, butter, and sugar in a bowl until crumbly. 2. Reserve 2 tablespoons of the mixture. 3. Press the remaining mixture firmly into the Easy-Bake Oven baking pan. 4. Spread with the jam. 5. Sprinkle the reserved mixture over the jam. Press gently with your fingers. 6. Bake in the Easy-Bake Oven for 18 minutes. 7. Cool, then cut into bars.

Serving Suggestion: Serve with fresh raspberries.

Variation Tip: Use your favorite type of jam.

Per Serving: Calories 197.3; Carbohydrates 21.5g; Protein 2.5g; Fat 11.6g; Sodium 59.8mg; Fiber 1g

Chapter 2 Breads and Pastries

Cherry Danish

Prep time: 20 minutes | Cook Time: 15 minutes | Serves: 4

Ingredients:

¼ cup baking mix
½ tablespoon margarine
¾ teaspoon sugar
4 teaspoons milk
½ tablespoon cherry pie filling

Preparation:

1. Combine the baking mix, margarine, and sugar in a bowl. Mix until crumbly. 2. Stir in the milk and mix until a dough forms. Beat the dough with 15 strokes. 3. Drop ½ teaspoonful onto the prepared baking pan. Indent each drop by pressing a thumb into 4. the middle. Fill each indent with cherry pie filling.5. Bake in the Easy-Bake Oven for 15 minutes or until golden brown.
Serving Suggestion: Serve with a drizzle of frosting on top.
Variation Tip: Brush a bit of melted butter on top before baking to enhance the flavor.
Per Serving: Calories 58; Carbohydrates 6g; Protein 3g; Fat 4g; Sodium 80mg; Fiber 1g; Sugars 2g

Cornbread

Prep time: 5 minutes | Cook Time: 15 minutes | Serves: 2

Ingredients:

1 tablespoon white sugar
2 teaspoons butter, softened
¼ teaspoon vanilla extract
¼ cup all-purpose flour
½ teaspoon baking powder
1 tablespoon cornmeal
2 tablespoons milk

Preparation:

1. In a small bowl, beat together the sugar, salt, butter, and vanilla until creamy. Add the milk and stir to combine. 2. In a separate bowl, mix together the flour, baking powder, and cornmeal. 3. Stir the flour mixture into the sugar mixture. 4. Put the batter into a greased and floured Easy-Bake Oven baking pan. 5. Bake in the Easy-Bake Oven for 15 minutes. Allow the cornbread to cool before serving.
Serving Suggestion: Spread some butter on top.
Variation Tip: You can add raisins for taste.
Per Serving: Calories 155.5; Carbohydrates 24.8g; Protein 3g; Fat 5.4g; Sodium 193.7mg; Fiber 1g

Blueberry Danish

Prep time: 5 minutes | Cook Time: 5 minutes | Serves: 2

Ingredients:

¼ cup baking mix
½ tablespoon margarine
¾ teaspoon sugar
4 teaspoons milk
½ tablespoon blueberry pie filling

For the frosting:

¼ cup powdered sugar
1 teaspoon water
2 drops vanilla extract

Preparation:

1. Combine the baking mix, margarine, and sugar in a bowl. Mix until crumbly. Add the milk and stir well until a soft dough forms. 2. Drop ½ teaspoonfuls onto a lightly greased Easy-Bake Oven baking pan. Indent each drop by pressing your thumb into the middle. Fill each indent with blueberry pie filling. 3. Bake in the Easy-Bake Oven until golden brown (about 5 minutes). 4. To make the frosting: Combine all the frosting ingredients in a bowl, mixing until it reaches a smooth consistency.

Serving Suggestion: Serve topped with the sugar frosting.

Variation Tip: This Danish also tastes good using a strawberry filling.

Per Serving: Calories 280; Carbohydrates 40g; Protein 4g; Fat 12g; Sodium 200mg; Fiber 1g

Ham & Cheese Bagel

Prep time: 5 minutes | Cook Time: 5 minutes | Serves: 1

Ingredients:

1 slice deli ham
1 bagel, cut in half
4 tablespoons cheese, softened

Preparation:

1. Toast the bagel halves. 2. Place the ham slice on top of one of the toasted bagel halves. 3. Put the cheese into an Easy-Bake Oven-safe cup. Cover with foil and place in the oven until melted. 4. Drizzle the warm cheese on top of the ham. Cover with the other toasted bagel half.

Serving Suggestion: Serve warm.

Variation Tip: You can use any type of cheese you prefer.

Per Serving: Calories 412; Carbohydrates 64.3g; Protein 16.1g; Fat 10.1g; Sodium 895mg; Fiber 2g

Cheese Twists

Prep time: 5 minutes | Cook Time: 10 minutes | Serves: 2

Ingredients:

8-ounce can refrigerator crescent rolls
2 teaspoons butter, melted
½ cup cheese, grated
Pinch of garlic salt

Preparation:

1. Divide the crescent roll dough in half. 2. Cut each dough half into a rectangle. Press perforations to seal. 3. Brush the first rectangle with butter, then sprinkle with cheese and garlic salt. 4. Place the second rectangle of dough on top of the first. 5. Cut into ½-inch strips. 6. Twist each strip five times. Squeeze the ends to seal. 7. Place the twists onto an ungreased Easy-Bake Oven baking pan and bake in the Easy-Bake Oven until golden brown (about 10 minutes).
Serving Suggestion: Serve warm.
Variation Tip: You can use mozzarella sticks for chewiness.
Per Serving: Calories 98; Carbohydrates 7.1g; Protein 1.3g; Fat 6.5g; Sodium 154.6mg; Fiber 0g

Scones

Prep time: 5 minutes | Cook Time: 15 minutes | Serves: 2

Ingredients:

1 tablespoon sour cream
⅛ teaspoon baking soda
⅓ cup all-purpose flour
1 tablespoon sugar
⅛ teaspoon baking powder
⅛ teaspoon cream of tartar
⅛ teaspoon salt
1 tablespoon butter
1 tablespoon raisins

Preparation:

1. Grease and flour the Easy-Bake Oven baking pan. 2. Blend the sour cream and baking soda in a small bowl, then set aside. 3. Mix together the flour, sugar, baking powder, cream of tartar, and salt. Cut in the butter. 4. Stir in the sour cream mixture until just moistened. Mix in the raisins. 5. Knead the dough briefly on a lightly floured surface. 6. Roll or pat the dough into ½-inch thick rounds. Cut into wedges and place them on the prepared baking sheet. 7. Bake in the Easy-Bake Oven for 15 minutes. 8. Let the scones cool before serving.
Serving Suggestion: Serve with your favorite jam.
Variation Tip: Add some whipping cream for a milkier flavor.
Per Serving: Calories 143.8; Carbohydrates 20.3; Protein 2.6g; Fat 5.8g; Sodium 196.4mg; Fiber 0.5g

Teacakes

Prep time: 5 minutes | Cook Time: 8 minutes | Serves: 12

Ingredients:

¼ cup all-purpose flour
¼ teaspoon baking powder
⅛ teaspoon salt
2 teaspoons sugar
2 teaspoons margarine
4 teaspoons milk
1 teaspoon multi-colored cookie decorations

Preparation:

1. Cream together the flour, baking powder, salt, sugar, and margarine until the dough looks like medium-sized crumbs. Slowly mix in the milk. 2. Place a few pieces of teaspoon-sized dough on a greased Easy-Bake Oven baking pan. 3. Sprinkle the cookie decorations over the top of the dough. 4. Bake in the Easy-Bake Oven for 8 minutes.

Serving Suggestion: Serve with tea.

Variation Tip: You can add raisins and orange zest for flavor.

Per Serving: Calories 89.5; Carbohydrates 4.1g; Protein 0.2g; Fat 8.3g; Sodium 50.4mg; Fiber 0.2g

Strawberry Danish

Prep time: 10 minutes | Cook Time: 15 minutes | Serves: 6

Ingredients:

¼ cup baking mix
½ tablespoon margarine
¾ teaspoon sugar
4 teaspoons milk
½ tablespoon strawberry pie filling

Preparation:

1. Combine the baking mix, margarine, and sugar in a bowl. Mix until crumbly. 2. Add the milk and stir well until a soft dough forms. 3. Drop ½ teaspoonful onto the lightly greased baking pan. Indent each by pressing your thumb into their middle. Fill each indent with the strawberry pie filling. 4. Bake in the Easy-Bake Oven for 15 minutes or until golden brown.

Serving Suggestion: Serve with some fresh strawberries and frosting on top.

Variation Tip: You can add cream to it when serving to enhance the flavor.

Per Serving: Calories 98; Fat 6.7g; Sodium 101mg; Carbohydrates 12.8g; Fiber 2.8g; Sugars 2g; Protein 2.2g

Chapter 3 Cakes and Brownies

Coconut Cream Pudding Cake

Prep time: 15 minutes | Cook Time: 15 minutes | Serves: 8

Ingredients:

2 tablespoons milk
1 package yellow cake mix
3 tablespoons coconut cream pudding mix
Anti-sticking baking spray
1 teaspoon coconut, shredded

Preparation:

1. Plug in the easy bake oven, preheating it for 15 minutes. 2. Spray the Easy-Bake Oven baking pan with baking spray and then dust lightly with flour. 3. Put all the ingredients into medium-sized bowl except coconut and whisk to incorporate. 4. Drizzle this mixture into the pan, and then dust coconut on top. 5. Lay out the mixture onto the baking pan. 6. Bake in the preheated oven for 15 minutes. 7. After cooking time is finished, with pan pusher, shove the baking pan into the "Cooling Chamber". 8. Give it about five minutes to cool down. 9. Turn the cake carefully onto a dish so it can cool completely before serving.

Per Serving: Calories 293; Fat 7.9g; Sodium 449mg; Carbs 52.7g; Fiber 0.8g; Sugar 28.6g; Protein 3.2g

Cocoa Brownie

Prep time: 10 minutes | Cook Time: 12 minutes | Serves: 12

Ingredients:

1 tablespoon water
2 tablespoons flour
Anti-sticking baking spray
1 tablespoon olive oil
2 tablespoons sugar
½ teaspoon vanilla
1 tablespoon cocoa powder

Preparation:

1. Plug in the easy bake oven, preheating it for 15 minutes. 2. Spritz baking spray on the baking pan, followed by dusting with flour. 3. In a bowl, merge cocoa powder with all other ingredients and whisk to incorporate. 4. Lay batter onto the baking pan. 5. Bake in the preheated oven for 12 minutes. 5. After cooking time is finished, give it about five minutes to cool down. 6. Carefully turn the brownies onto a platter to serve and enjoy.

Per Serving: Calories 48; Fat 2.4g; Sodium 0mg; Carbs 6.5g; Fiber 0.3g; Sugar 4.1g; Protein 0.4g

Cinnamon Cake

Prep time: 15 minutes | Cook Time: 15 minutes | Serves: 6

Ingredients:

¼ teaspoon cinnamon
⅛ egg, slightly beaten
Anti-sticking baking spray
⅓ cup all-purpose biscuit baking mix
1 tablespoon milk
2½ teaspoons white sugar
1 teaspoon vegetable oil

Preparation:

1. Plug in the easy bake oven, preheating it for 15 minutes. 2. Spritz baking spray on the baking pan, followed by dusting with flour. 3. Merge all the ingredients into medium-sized bowl. 4. Whisk thoroughly to incorporate. 5. Lay out the mixture onto the baking pan about 1½-inch apart. 6. Bake in the preheated oven for 15 minutes. 7. After cooking time is finished, with pan pusher, shove the baking pan into the "Cooling Chamber". 8. Give it about five minutes to cool down. 9. Turn off the oven and with a spatula, take off the baking pan from oven. 10. Shift the baking pan on a countertop to cool down for approximately five minutes. 11. Carefully turn the cinnamon coffee cake onto a platter to serve and enjoy.

Per Serving: Calories 26; Fat 1.2g; Sodium 31mg; Carbs 3.5g; Fiber 0.1g; Sugar 2g; Protein 0.4g

Multi Colored Tea Cakes

Prep time: 15 minutes | Cook Time: 12 minutes | Serves: 8

Ingredients:

⅛ teaspoon salt
1 teaspoon multi colored cookie decorations
2 teaspoons sugar
Anti-sticking baking spray
2 teaspoons margarine
¼ teaspoon baking powder
¼ cup flour, all-purpose
4 teaspoons milk

Preparation:

1. Plug in the easy bake oven, preheating it for 15 minutes. 2. Spritz baking spray on the baking pan, followed by dusting with flour. 3. Merge the flour with baking powder, salt, margarine, and sugar to form a crumbly mixture. 4. Gradually incorporate the milk into the mixture, stirring slowly. 5. Sprinkle cookie decorations over the top of each dough portion. 6. Lay small teaspoon-sized portions of the dough onto the baking pan. 7. Bake in the preheated oven for 12 minutes. 8. After cooking time is finished, with pan pusher, shove the baking pan into the "Cooling Chamber". 9. Give it about five minutes to cool down. 10. Then carefully turn the tea cakes onto a platter to serve and enjoy.

Per Serving: Calories 52; Fat 2g; Sodium 58mg; Carbs 7.7g; Fiber 0.2g; Sugar 2.4g; Protein 0.7g

Chocolate Brownies with Mint Frosting

Prep time: 15 minutes | Cook Time: 15 minutes | Serves: 6

Ingredients:

2 tablespoons white sugar
Anti-sticking baking spray
2 tablespoons flour, all-purpose
3 tablespoons chocolate syrup
1 tablespoon butter

Frosting:
½ teaspoon peppermint extract
¼ cup confectioners' sugar
½ cup butter

Preparation:

1. Plug in the easy bake oven, preheating it for 15 minutes. 2. Spritz baking spray on the baking pan, followed by dusting with flour. 3. Put sugars and butter into medium-sized bowl and whisk to incorporate. 4. Fold in the chocolate syrup and flour and whisk to incorporate thoroughly. 5. Lay out batter onto the baking pan about 1½-inch apart. 6. Lay out the pan into the "Baking Slot" of Easy-Bake Ultimate Oven. 7. With pan pusher, shove baking pan into the "Baking Chamber". 8. Set the cooking time for 15 minutes. 9. After cooking time is finished, with pan pusher, shove the baking pan into the "Cooling Chamber". 10. Give it about five minutes to cool down. 11. Turn off the oven and with a spatula, take off the baking pan from oven. 12. Cook the remnant cookies in the same way. 13. Merge the frosting ingredients thoroughly and spread over the brownies before enjoying.

Per Serving: Calories 207; Fat 15.5g; Sodium 116mg; Carbs 17.1g; Fiber 0.3g; Sugar 8.7g; Protein 0.6g

White Chocolate Mix

Prep time: 10 minutes | Cook Time: 12–15 minutes | Serves: 2

Ingredients:

1 package yellow cake mix
3 tablespoons white chocolate pudding mix
2 tablespoons plus 1 teaspoon milk

Preparation:

1. Mix the cake mix, pudding mix, and milk in a bowl. Stir until the batter is smooth. 2. Pour the batter into the Easy-Bake Oven baking pan. You'll need to bake in batches. 3. Bake each batch in the Easy-Bake Oven for 12–15 minutes or until the sides of the cake separate from the pan. 4. Remove and allow to cool completely.

Serving Suggestion: Decorate with mini white chocolate chips and vanilla frosting.

Variation Tip: You can also top the cake with fresh fruit, whipped cream, or meringue.

Per Serving: Calories 477; Fat 19.4g; Sodium 424.4mg; Carbohydrates 72g; Fiber 1.5g; Sugars 49.9g; Protein 4.1g

Blueberry Shortcake with Cool Whip

Prep time: 15 minutes | Cook Time: 10 minutes | Serves: 6

Ingredients:

1 tablespoon sugar
3 tablespoons cool whip
Anti-sticking baking spray
¼ cup biscuit mix
5 teaspoons milk
⅛ teaspoon cinnamon
¼ cup blueberries

Preparation:

1. Plug in the easy bake oven, preheating it for 15 minutes. 2. Spritz baking spray on the baking pan, followed by dusting with flour. 3. Use a fork to combine the biscuit mix and milk until well blended. 4. Split the mixture into two portions that are equal in size. 5. Roll out one portion at a time to match the size of the pan. 6. In a separate bowl, mingle blueberries, cinnamon, and sugar, keeping aside. 7. Lay out the rolled-out portion onto the baking pan. 8. Bake in the preheated oven for 10 minutes. 9. After cooking time is finished, with pan pusher, shove the baking pan into the "Cooling Chamber". 10. Give it about five minutes to cool down. 11. Carefully turn the cake onto a platter to cool and top with blueberries and Cool Whip.

Per Serving: Calories 43; Fat 1.4g; Sodium 63mg; Carbs 7.4g; Fiber 0.4g; Sugar 4.3g; Protein 0.6g

Pretty Rose Cake

Prep time: 10 minutes | Cook Time: 25 minutes | Serves: 3

Ingredients:

1½ cups all-purpose flour
¾ cup powdered sugar
2 teaspoons baking powder
½ cup milk
¼ cup cooking oil
¼ cup + 1 tablespoon of Rose syrup
1/3 teaspoon rose essence

Preparation:

1. Mix all the dry ingredients in a bowl. 2. In a separate bowl, mix all the liquid ingredients. 3. Combine the ingredients of both bowls together. 4. Pour the batter into the prepared baking pan. 5. Bake for 25 minutes or until a toothpick inserted into the center of the cake comes out clean. 6. Allow the cake to cool before serving.

Serving Suggestion: Serve with milk.

Variation Tip: None, this cake is delicious as it is!

Per Serving: Calories 601; Fat 19.6g; Sodium 23mg; Carbs 101g; Fiber 1.8g; Sugar 52.1g; Protein 7.8g

Devil's Food Cake

Prep time: 15 minutes | Cook Time: 15 minutes | Serves: 8

Ingredients:

1 package yellow cake mix
2 tablespoons milk
3 tablespoons pudding mix, Devil's food
Anti-sticking baking spray

Preparation:

1. Plug in the easy bake oven, preheating it for 15 minutes. 2. Spray the Easy-Bake Oven baking pan with baking spray and then dust lightly with flour. 3. Put all the ingredients into medium-sized bowl and whisk to incorporate. 4. Drizzle the mixture into the prepared pan. 5. Lay out the mixture onto the baking pan. 6. Bake in the preheated oven for 15 minutes. 7. After cooking time is finished, with pan pusher, shove the baking pan into the "Cooling Chamber". 8. Give it about five minutes to cool down. 9. Turn the cake carefully onto a dish so it can cool completely before serving.
Per Serving: Calories 289; Fat 7.7g; Sodium 456mg; Carbs 52.4g; Fiber 0.8g; Sugar 28.6g; Protein 3g

Easy Lemon Cake

Prep time: 15 minutes | Cook Time: 15 minutes | Serves: 10

Ingredients:

1 teaspoon baking soda
Anti-sticking baking spray
½ teaspoon salt
4 teaspoons water
1 teaspoon lemonade drink mix, unsweetened
1½ cups flour, all-purpose
1 cup sugar

Preparation:

1. Plug in the easy bake oven, preheating it for 15 minutes. 2. Spritz baking spray on the baking pan, followed by dusting with flour. 3. Merge sugar with baking soda, lemonade drink mix, flour, and salt in a bowl and whisk to incorporate. 4. Place approximately ⅓ cup mixture into ten small plastic bags. 5. In a small bowl, empty the contents of a single bag of cake mix. 6. Then, blend it with water until smooth. 7. Lay out the mixture onto the baking pan. 8. Bake in the preheated oven for 15 minutes. 9. After cooking time is finished, with pan pusher, shove the baking pan into the "Cooling Chamber". 10. Give it about five minutes to cool down. 11. Turn off the oven and with a spatula, take off the baking pan from oven. 12. Cook the remnant cake mix in the same way. 13. Turn the cake carefully onto a dish so it can cool completely before serving.
Per Serving: Calories 143; Fat 0.2g; Sodium 244mg; Carbs 34.3g; Fiber 0.5g; Sugar 20.1g; Protein 1.9g

Vanilla Pudding Cake

Prep time: 15 minutes | Cook Time: 15 minutes | Serves: 8

Ingredients:

2 tablespoons milk
Anti-sticking baking spray
3 tablespoons French vanilla pudding mix
1 package yellow cake mix

Preparation:

1. Plug in the easy bake oven, preheating it for 15 minutes. 2. Spray the Easy-Bake Oven baking pan with baking spray and then dust lightly with flour. 3. In a bowl, merge the cake mix with pudding mix and milk and whisk to incorporate. 4. Trickle the mixture into the prepared baking pan. 5. Bake in the preheated oven for 15 minutes. 6. After cooking time is finished, with pan pusher, shove the baking pan into the "Cooling Chamber". 7. Give it about five minutes to cool down. 8. Turn off the oven and with a spatula, take off the baking pan from oven. 9. Shift the baking pan on a countertop to cool down for approximately five minutes. 10. Turn the cake carefully onto a dish so it can cool completely before serving.

Per Serving: Calories 296; Fat 8.2g; Sodium 452mg; Carbs 51.9g; Fiber 1.1g; Sugar 28.6g; Protein 4.3g

Easy Baked Alaska

Prep time: 10 minutes (plus 4 hours for freezing) | Cook Time: 20 minutes | Serves: 3

Ingredients:

3 cups Neapolitan ice cream, slightly softened
½-pound cake, sliced into 1-inch-thick pieces
3 egg whites
½ teaspoon cream of tartar
¾ cup sugar

Preparation:

1. Take a bowl and line it with plastic wrap. 2. Scoop the ice cream into the bowl. Press it in to make sure no spaces are showing. 3. Top the ice cream with the pound cake slices, cutting them if necessary to ensure the ice cream is completely covered. 4. Gently press the cake into the ice cream. 5. Cover and freeze for 3 hours. 6. When the cake is frozen, beat together the egg whites and cream of tartar. 7. Once smooth, add the sugar and beat until stiff peaks form. 8. Invert the frozen cake onto the baking pan. Remove the plastic wrap. 9. Cover the cake with the meringue and freeze for at least 1 hour. 10. Bake the cake for 5 minutes, or until the meringue is golden.

Serving Suggestion: Serve sliced with whipped cream.

Variation Tip: None, this recipe is yummy!

Per Serving: Calories 618; Fat 18g; Sodium 349mg; Carbs 111g; Fiber 0.2g; Sugar 62g; Protein 8.3g

Chocolate Lava Cake

Prep time: 10 minutes | Cook Time: 15 minutes | Serves: 2

Ingredients:

1⁄3 cup butter
1⁄3 cup semi-sweet chocolate chips
¾ cup powdered sugar
2 eggs
6 tablespoons cornstarch

Preparation:

1. Place two greased ramekins on the oven's baking pan. 2. Put the chocolate chips and butter in a microwave-safe bowl and heat in the microwave until melted. 3. Add the sugar and stir well. 4. Add in the eggs and combine until smooth. 5. Add the cornstarch and stir well. 6. Divide the batter between the ramekins. 7. Bake for 15 minutes.
Serving Suggestion: Serve with vanilla ice cream.
Variation Tip: None, this recipe is delicious!
Per Serving: Calories 776; Fat 45.1g; Sodium 282mg; Carbs 89.9g; Fiber 2.7g; Sugar 54.4g; Protein 8.4g

Strawberry Shortcake

Prep time: 10 minutes | Cook Time: 10 minutes | Serves: 2

Ingredients:

¼ cup baking mix
5 teaspoons milk
4 strawberries, sliced, for decoration
Whipped topping, as required, for decoration

Preparation:

1. Combine the baking mix and milk in a bowl using a fork. 2. Divide the batter into two portions. Put one portion into the prepared baking pan. 3. Bake in the Easy-Bake Oven for about 10 minutes. Let it cool. Repeat for the remaining batter. 4. Top with the strawberries and whipped topping.
Serving Suggestion: Serve with vanilla ice cream.
Variation Tip: You can add a drop of red food coloring to the batter.
Per Serving: Calories 125; Carbohydrates 15g; Protein 4g; Fat 5g; Sodium 123 mg; Fiber 3g; Sugars 2g

Pot of Gold

Prep time: 10 minutes | Cook Time: 10 minutes | Serves: 1

Ingredients:

2 devil's food cake mixes
White frosting mix
Yellow food coloring
Yellow crystal sugar sprinkles.
Chocolate fingers
2 chocolate kisses
Chocolate coins
Sprinkles/colored candy of your choice

Preparation:

1. Bake the cake mixes according to the packet directions. You'll need to bake the mixes in batches. Once cooked, let the cakes cool completely. 2. While the cakes are baking, prepare the white frosting. Add a drop of yellow food coloring to make it a "gold" color. 3. When cooled, layer the cakes on top of each other, using some of the frosting to "glue" them together. 4. Spread the remaining frosting around the sides and top of the cake. Sprinkle with the yellow crystal sugar sprinkles for the "gold.". 5. Arrange the chocolate fingers around the cake. Press gently, so they stick to the frosting. 6. Add the chocolate coins and any other colored candy of your choice to the top. 7. Enjoy your pot of gold!

Serving Suggestion: Serve as a birthday treat.

Variation Tip: You can use lots of different toppings.

Per Serving: Calories 364.4; Fat 20.6g; Sodium 321.6mg; Carbohydrates 40.6g; Fiber 0.6g; Sugars 23.6g; Protein 5g

Red Velvet Cake

Prep time: 15 minutes | Cook Time: 15 minutes | Serves: 2

Ingredients:

3 tablespoons flour
1⁄6 teaspoon baking soda
Dash of salt
1½ tablespoons red sugar crystals
1⁄6 teaspoon vanilla
3 teaspoons vegetable oil
6 teaspoons milk
Pink frosting or buttercream, for decoration

Preparation:

1. Mix the cake flour, red sugar crystals, vanilla, oil, milk, salt, and baking soda in a bowl. 2. Mix it into a smooth batter. 3. Pour the batter into the prepared baking pan. 4. Bake for 15 minutes 5. Frost it with the frosting or buttercream.

Serving Suggestion: Serve the cake with ice cream.

Variation Tip: You can use red food coloring instead of red sugar crystals.

Per Serving: Calories 146; Fat 7.2g; Sodium 95mg; Carbs 17.3g; Fiber 0.3g; Sugar 8.1g; Protein 1.7g

Toffee Trifle Cake

Prep time: 10 minutes | Cook Time: 15minutes | Serves: 2–3

Ingredients:

8 tablespoons yellow cake mix
3 tablespoons milk
1 small box instant pudding mix, vanilla flavor
11⁄3 cups cold milk
1 cup Cool Whip
2 candy bars, crushed

Preparation:

1. Combine the yellow cake mix and milk in a bowl. Mix until smooth. 2. Pour the mixture into the prepared baking pan and bake for 15 minutes. 3. Let the cake cool completely, and then cut it into small cubes. 4. Whisk together the cold milk and pudding mix. 5. Fold in the Cool Whip. 6. Take two or three glass bowls, and start arranging the pieces of cake in the bottom of each. 7. Cover with a generous amount of pudding mixture, and then sprinkle on some of the crushed candy. 8. Repeat the layers until all the ingredients are used. 9. Refrigerate for 2 hours before serving.

Serving Suggestion: Top with some more Cool Whip and chocolate shavings.
Variation Tip: Use any kind of candy bar you like.
Per Serving: Calories 220; Fat 12.1g; Sodium 142mg; Carbs 25.6g; Fiber 0.6g; Sugar 18.3g; Protein 2.9g

Party Cake

Prep time: 10 minutes | Cook Time: 10 minutes | Serves: 2

Ingredients:

½ cup all-purpose flour
½ teaspoon baking powder
¼ teaspoon salt
4 teaspoons sugar
4 teaspoons margarine
8 teaspoons milk
Multi-colored cookie decorations.

Preparation:

1. Take a bowl and add the flour, baking powder, sugar, margarine, and salt. 2. Combine well, and then add in the milk. 3. Once the batter is ready, pour it into the prepared baking pan. 4. Sprinkle the top of the batter with the cookie decorations. 5. Bake for about 10 minutes or until a toothpick inserted into the center of the cake comes out clean.

Serving Suggestion: Allow the cake to cool completely, and then add frosting or buttercream of your choice.
Variation Tip: Use butter instead of margarine.
Per Serving: Calories 443; Fat 16.3g; Sodium 479mg; Carbs 67.5g; Fiber 0.9g; Sugar 25g; Protein 6g

Coconut Cream Cake

Prep time: 10 minutes | Cook Time: 12–15 minutes | Serves: 1

Ingredients:

1 package yellow cake mix
2 tablespoons milk
3 tablespoons coconut cream pudding mix
1 teaspoon shredded coconut

Preparation:

1. Combine all the ingredients in a small bowl except the shredded coconut. Mix until the batter is smooth. 2. Pour half of the batter into the prepared baking pan. (You will bake the second half next.) Sprinkle ½ teaspoon of the shredded coconut on top. 3. Bake in the Easy-Bake Oven for 12 to 15 minutes or until the sides separate from the pan. 4. Remove and allow to cool completely. Repeat for the rest of the batter.

Serving Suggestion: Serve the cake with coconut frosting.

Variation Tip: Sprinkle dried fruits and nuts on the cake.

Per Serving: Calories 416; Carbohydrates 67g; Protein 4g; Fat 15g; Sodium 300mg; Fiber 1g; Sugars 46g

Banana Cream Cake

Prep time: 5 minutes | Cook Time: 15 minutes | Serves: 3

Ingredients:

6 tablespoons flour
4 teaspoons sugar
¼ teaspoon baking powder
Dash of salt
6 teaspoons milk
2 teaspoons shortening
3 tablespoons banana cream pudding mix
Frosting of choice

Preparation:

1. Grease and flour the Easy-Bake Oven baking pan. 2. Mix the flour, sugar, baking powder, and salt in a bowl. Add the milk and shortening. Stir until the batter is smooth, then add the banana cream pudding mix. 3. Pour the batter into the prepared pan. Bake in the Easy-Bake Oven for 12 to 15 minutes or until the sides of the cake separate from the pan. 4. Remove the cake and cool. Frost with your choice of frosting.

Serving Suggestion: Serve topped with whipped cream and banana slices.

Variation Tip: You can add in some mini chocolate chips.

Per Serving: Calories 251.8; Carbohydrates 33.7g; Protein 2.6g; Fat 12.3g; Sodium 185.7mg; Fiber 0.6g

Barbie's Pretty Pink Cake

Prep time: 5 minutes | Cook Time: 15 minutes | Serves: 2

Ingredients:

4½ tablespoons all-purpose flour
¼ teaspoon baking powder
⅛ teaspoon salt
4 teaspoons red sugar crystals
¼ teaspoon vanilla extract
4 teaspoons vegetable oil
8 teaspoons milk

Preparation:

1. Stir together the flour, baking powder, salt, red sugar crystals, vanilla, oil, and milk until the batter is smooth and pink. 2. Pour 3 tablespoons of the batter into a greased and floured Easy-Bake Oven baking pan. Bake for 15 minutes in the Easy-Bake Oven. Repeat to make the second layer. 3. Allow the cake layers to cool completely, then sandwich them together with your choice of frosting or buttercream colored with a drop of red food coloring. Top with frosting or buttercream.

Serving Suggestion: Serve with vanilla ice cream.

Variation Tip: Sprinkle some colorful cake sprinkles on top.

Per Serving: Calories 39.55; Carbohydrates 4.12g; Protein 0.6g; Fat 2.31g; Sodium 114.32mg; Fiber 0.4g

Banana Trifle Cake

Prep time: 5 minutes | Cook Time: 15 minutes | Serves: 2

Ingredients:

6 tablespoons yellow cake mix
2 tablespoons milk
3 tablespoons banana pudding
3 tablespoons whipped cream
¼ banana, sliced

Preparation:

1. Mix the yellow cake mix with 2 tablespoons of milk in a bowl until smooth. 2. Pour the batter into a greased Easy-Bake Oven baking pan (you may need to bake in batches) and bake in the Easy-Bake Oven for about 15. 3. Let the cake cool. Cut it into small squares. 4. Mix the pudding and whipped cream together in a bowl. 5. Arrange half of the cake pieces in the bottom of a mini trifle dish or small glass bowl. Cover with some of the pudding mixture. 6. Add some sliced banana. 7. Repeat layering until all the ingredients are used. 8. Chill until serving.

Serving Suggestion: Serve with a sprinkling of shaved chocolate on top.

Variation Tip: You can add some sliced almonds for crunch.

Per Serving: Calories 407.8; Carbohydrates 49.3g; Protein 4.3g; Fat 11.3g; Sodium 484.2mg; Fiber 0.5g

Birthday Cake

Prep time: 5 minutes | Cook Time: 15 minutes | Serves: 1

Ingredients:

4 teaspoons flour
2 teaspoons cocoa powder
1 tablespoon sugar
⅛ teaspoon baking powder
Dash of salt
⅛ teaspoon vanilla extract
4 teaspoons water
2 teaspoons vegetable oil
Frosting of your choice

Preparation:

1. Combine all the ingredients except for the frosting in a small bowl. Stir until the batter is smooth and chocolate-colored. 2. Pour the batter into a greased and floured Easy-Bake baking pan. 3. Bake in the Easy-Bake Oven for 13 to 15 minutes or until the cake pulls away from the sides of the pan. 4. Remove the cake from the oven and cool.

Serving Suggestion: Serve topped with your favorite frosting.

Variation Tip: You can also add some mini chocolate chips.

Per Serving: Calories 321.2; Carbohydrates 49.3g; Protein 3.4g; Fat 12.73g; Sodium 82mg; Fiber 0.4g

Black Forest Cake

Prep time: 5 minutes | Cook Time: 24 minutes | Serves: 2

Ingredients:

2 chocolate cake mixes
6 teaspoons water
Cherry pie filling
Whipped cream

Preparation:

1. Pour the contents of one of the cake mixes into a mixing bowl. Add 3 teaspoons of water and mix until smooth. 2. Pour evenly into a greased Easy-Bake Oven baking pan. 3. Bake in Easy-Bake Oven for 12 minutes. (While that cake is baking, prepare the second cake mix, then bake when the first has baked and cooled.) 4. Allow the cake to cool in the cooling chamber for 10 minutes before removing it. 5. Place the first cake onto a serving plate. 6. Place some cherry pie filling on top. 7. Place the second cake on top of the first and add a layer of cherry pie filling. 8. Add some whipped cream on the top and sides of the layered cake.

Serving Suggestion: Serve with some glacé cherries on top.

Variation Tip: Add some toasted almonds for flavor.

Per Serving: Calories 270; Carbohydrates 38g; Protein 3g; Fat 12g; Sodium 250mg; Fiber 1g

Blueberry Shortcake

Prep time: 5 minutes | Cook Time: 10 minutes | Serves: 2

Ingredients:

¼ cup biscuit mix
5 teaspoons milk
6 blueberries
1 tablespoon sugar
⅛ teaspoon ground cinnamon

Preparation:

1. Combine the biscuit mix and milk in a bowl using a fork. 2. Divide the mixture into two portions. 3. Roll out the portions one at a time on a floured surface so that each can fit in the Easy-Bake Oven baking pan. 4. Grease the baking pan and put the two portions in it. 5. Bake in the Easy-Bake Oven for about 10 minutes. 6. Allow the shortcake to cool. 7. In a bowl, mix the blueberries, cinnamon, and sugar.

Serving Suggestion: Top with the blueberry mixture and some whipped cream.

Variation Tip: Add some sliced fresh blueberries to the biscuit mix for taste.

Per Serving: Calories 120; Carbohydrates 16g; Protein 1g; Fat 6g; Sodium 60mg; Fiber 2g

Cherry Cheesecake

Prep time: 5 minutes | Cook Time: 20 minutes | Serves: 2

Ingredients:

1 packet sugar cookie dough
2 tablespoons cherry pie filling

For the cream cheese filling:

2 tablespoons cream cheese
2 teaspoons powdered sugar

Preparation:

1. Press the cookie dough evenly into the Easy-Bake Oven baking pan. 2. Bake for 15 to 20 minutes or until golden brown. 3. Cool in the pan on a wire rack. 4. Mix the cream cheese with the powdered sugar in a large mixing bowl to make the cream cheese filling. 5. Spread the cream cheese mixture onto the cooled cookie dough. Cover with the cherry pie filling.

Serving Suggestion: Serve in slices and enjoy.

Variation Tip: You can also use some fresh cherries.

Per Serving: Calories 181.5; Carbohydrates 23.4g; Protein 5.1g; Fat 3g; Sodium 266 mg; Fiber 0g

Carrot Cake

Prep time: 5 minutes | Cook Time: 20 minutes | Serves: 3

Ingredients:

2 yellow cake mixes
⅛ teaspoon ground cinnamon
2 pinches ground nutmeg
2 pinches ground ginger
1 tablespoon carrots, shredded
2 teaspoons canned pineapple, drained and crushed
1 teaspoon egg, beaten
2½ teaspoons water
Cream cheese frosting, for serving

Preparation:

1. Grease and flour the Easy-Bake Oven baking pan. 2. Combine all the ingredients except for the frosting in a bowl until thoroughly mixed. 3. Pour half of the mixture into the baking pan. You'll need to bake in batches. 4. Bake each batch in the Easy-Bake Oven for 9 minutes each. 5. Remove the cake from the pan and allow it to cool completely. 6. Apply cream cheese frosting between the cake layers and around the cake.

Serving Suggestion: Serve with a sprinkling of ground cinnamon.

Variation Tip: You can also add some banana slices to the batter for flavor enhancement.

Per Serving: Calories 577; Carbohydrates 73g; Protein 6.6g; Fat 30g; Sodium 415mg; Fiber 1.6g

Chocolate Cake

Prep time: 5 minutes | Cook Time: 15 minutes | Serves: 2

Ingredients:

6 teaspoons flour
4 teaspoons sugar
¼ teaspoon baking powder
1 teaspoon unsweetened cocoa
¾ teaspoon shortening
Pinch of salt
6 teaspoons milk

Preparation:

1. Mix the flour, sugar, baking powder, cocoa, shortening, and salt in a bowl. Add the milk and combine well. 2. Pour the mixture into a greased Easy-Bake Oven baking pan. 3. Bake in the Easy-Bake Oven for 12 to 15 minutes. 4. Allow the cake to cool before serving.

Serving Suggestion: Serve topped with melted chocolate.

Variation Tip: Add chocolate chunks to the batter for a richer flavor.

Per Serving: Calories 424; Carbohydrates 57.7g; Protein 3.8g; Fat 22g; Sodium 379mg; Fiber 2.4g

Cinnamon Coffee Cake

Prep time: 5 minutes | Cook Time: 15 minutes | Serves: 2

Ingredients:

⅓ cup all-purpose biscuit baking mix
2¾ teaspoons white sugar
1 teaspoon vegetable oil
⅛ egg, slightly beaten
¼ teaspoon ground cinnamon
1 tablespoon milk

Preparation:

1. Stir all the ingredients together until just moistened. 2. Pour the batter into a greased and floured Easy-Bake Oven baking pan. 3. Bake in the Easy-Bake Oven for 15 minutes. Let it cool before serving.
Serving Suggestion: Serve topped with powdered sugar.
Variation Tip: You can add some apple chunks for taste.
Per Serving: Calories 233; Carbohydrates 34g; Protein 2g; Fat 9g; Sodium 153mg; Fiber 1g

Peanut Butter Butterscotch Brownie

Prep time: 5 minutes | Cook Time: 20 minutes | Serves: 2

Ingredients:

2 tablespoons butter
¼ cube brown sugar
¼ cup flour
⅓ teaspoon baking powder
¼ teaspoon vanilla extract
1 tablespoon peanut butter
3 tablespoons mini butterscotch chips

Preparation:

1. Cream together the butter and brown sugar in a bowl. 2. In a small bowl, mix the flour and baking powder. Add it to the creamed butter/sugar mixture a little at a time, until well mixed. 3. Add the vanilla and peanut butter, mixing well. Add the mini butterscotch chips. 4. Spread the mixture into the greased Easy-Bake Oven baking pan. 5. Bake in the Easy-Bake Oven for 15 to 20 minutes.
Serving Suggestion: Serve with cold milk.
Variation Tip: You can use chopped pecans for garnish.
Per Serving: Calories 151; Carbohydrates 19.46g; Protein 1.85g; Fat 7.54g; Sodium 95mg; Fiber 0.4g

Chocolate Mint Brownies

Prep time: 5 minutes | Cook Time: 15 minutes | Serves: 2

Ingredients:

2 tablespoons white sugar
1 tablespoon butter, softened
3 tablespoons chocolate syrup
2 tablespoons all-purpose flour

For the frosting:

¼ cup powdered sugar
½ cup butter
½ teaspoon peppermint extract

Preparation:

1. Grease the Easy-Bake Oven baking pan. 2. Cream together the butter and white sugar until smooth. Stir in the chocolate syrup and flour until blended. 3. Spread the batter evenly into the prepared pan. 4. Bake in the Easy-Bake Oven for 15 minutes. Cool completely in the pan. 5. Beat the powdered sugar, ½ cup of butter, and peppermint extract until smooth. 6. Spread the frosting evenly over the cooled brownies, then chill until set

Serving Suggestion: Serve with cold milk.

Variation Tip: Add chocolate chunks for the richness of flavor.

Per Serving: Calories 238.3; Carbohydrates 34.4g; Protein 1.8g; Fat 11.2g; Sodium 87.9mg; Fiber 1g

Banana Chocolate Brownies

Prep time: 5 minutes | Cook Time: 20 minutes | Serves: 2

Ingredients:

1 tablespoon butter
1 tablespoon white sugar
1 tablespoon brown sugar
⅛ teaspoon vanilla extract
2 tablespoons banana, mashed
3 tablespoons all-purpose flour
¼ teaspoon baking powder
⅛ teaspoon salt
2 tablespoons semi-sweet chocolate chips

Preparation:

1. Grease and flour the Easy-Bake Oven baking pan. 2. In a small bowl, cream the butter and sugars until smooth. Beat in the egg and vanilla, then fold in the mashed banana. 3. In a separate bowl, mix the flour, baking powder, and salt. 4. Fold the flour mixture into the butter mixture, mixing well. Stir in the chocolate chips. 5. Spread the batter into the baking pan. 6. Bake in Easy-Bake Oven for 20 minutes, until set. Cool before cutting.

Serving Suggestion: Serve with whipped cream.

Variation Tip: You can use chopped nuts in the batter for crunch.

Per Serving: Calories 120; Carbohydrates 16g; Protein 1g; Fat 6g; Sodium 60mg; Fiber 2g

French Vanilla Cake

Prep time: 5 minutes | Cook Time: 15 minutes | Serves: 2

Ingredients:

3 tablespoons French vanilla pudding mix
2 tablespoons milk
1 pack yellow cake mix

Preparation:

1. Grease and flour an Easy-Bake Oven baking pan. 2. Combine the cake mix, pudding mix, and milk, stirring until the batter is smooth. 3. Pour half of the mixture into the baking pan. You'll need to cook in batches. 4. Bake in the Easy-Bake Oven for 12 to 15 minutes or until the sides separate from the pan. 5. Remove and cool. Repeat for the rest of the batter.
Serving Suggestion: Serve with a scoop of vanilla ice cream.
Variation Tip: Serve with raspberry jam on top.
Per Serving: Calories 201.5; Carbohydrates 25g; Protein 2.8g; Fat 10.2g; Sodium 62.7mg; Fiber 0.4g

Oreo Cookies 'N Creme Cake

Prep time: 5 minutes | Cook Time: 15 minutes | Serves: 2

Ingredients:

3 tablespoons Jell-O Oreo Cookies 'n Creme Instant Pudding Mix
2 tablespoons milk
1 pack yellow cake mix
1 teaspoon coconut, shredded

Preparation:

1. Grease and flour an Easy-Bake Oven baking pan. This recipe requires you to cook in 2 batches. 2. Combine the pudding mix, milk, and cake mix in a bowl, stirring until the batter is smooth. 3. Pour half of the batter into the prepared pan. Top with ½ teaspoon of shredded coconut. 4. Bake in the Easy-Bake Oven for 12 to 15 minutes or until the sides of the cake separate from the pan. 5. Remove and cool. 6. Repeat steps 3 to 5 for the rest of the batter.
Serving Suggestion: Serve with whipped cream on top.
Variation Tip: You can add some crushed Oreo biscuits for crunch.
Per Serving: Calories 440; Carbohydrates 70.7g; Protein 1g; Fat 19.8g; Sodium 259mg; Fiber 0.8g

Lemon Trifle Cake

Prep time: 5 minutes | Cook Time: 15 minutes | Serves: 2

Ingredients:

6 tablespoons yellow cake mix
2 tablespoons milk
1 small box lemon instant pudding mix
1½ cups cold milk
1 small tub Cool Whip, softened

Preparation:

1. Mix the yellow cake mix with 2 tablespoons of milk in a bowl until smooth. 2. Pour the mixture into an Easy-Bake Oven baking pan. You may need to bake in batches. 3. Bake in the Easy-Bake Oven for about 15 minutes. 4. Let the cake cool completely, then cut it into small bite-sized squares. 5. Repeat for the second batch. 6. Mix 1½ cups cold milk with the pudding mix. Fold in the Cool Whip. 7. In a trifle dish or glass bowl, arrange the pieces from one cake on the bottom. Cover with some pudding mixture. Repeat the layers. Repeat in another dish or bowl for the pieces of cake from the second batch. 8. Chill until served.

Serving Suggestion: Serve chilled.

Variation Tip: You can also make this kind of trifle using orange pudding mix.

Per Serving: Calories 297; Carbohydrates 48.3g; Protein 5g; Fat 10g; Sodium 578.3mg; Fiber 1g

Pink Velvet Cake

Prep time: 5 minutes | Cook Time: 15 minutes | Serves: 2

Ingredients:

5 tablespoons flour
¼ teaspoon baking powder
⅛ teaspoon salt
5 teaspoons red sugar crystals
¼ teaspoon vanilla
4 teaspoons vegetable oil
8 teaspoons milk
Frosting or buttercream of your choice

Preparation:

1. Stir together all the ingredients except for the frosting or buttercream in a large bowl until the batter is smooth and pink. 2. Pour 3 tablespoons of batter into the greased and floured Easy-Bake Oven baking pan. 3. Bake in the Easy-Bake Oven for 15 minutes. 4. Take the cake out of the oven and allow it to cool completely. Bake the remaining batter. 5. Sandwich the cake layers together using frosting or buttercream of your choice. Top with another layer of frosting or buttercream.

Serving Suggestion: Add colored cake decorations on top.

Variation Tip: You can use strawberry or raspberry jam instead of frosting.

Per Serving: Calories 130; Carbohydrates 25g; Protein 2g; Fat 16g; Sodium 160g; Fiber 1g

Rainbow Cake

Prep time: 5 minutes | Cook Time: 60 minutes | Serves: 2

Ingredients:

1 white cake mix
White frosting mix
Food coloring (red, blue, green, yellow)

Preparation:

1. Prepare the cake batter as per the packet instructions. Divide the batter into small batches. 2. Mix each batch with a different color food coloring to make batches of red, yellow, blue, and purple (red and blue) colored batter. 3. Bake each color separately in the Easy-Bake Oven baking pan for 15 minutes. 4. Cool the cakes for 10 minutes before removing them from the tin. Let the cakes cool completely.
To make the frosting: Mix three batches of frosting with food coloring to make small amounts of orange (red and yellow), green, and indigo (red and blue) frosting. Make sure you have some white frosting left.
To assemble the cake: Layer the cake and frosting as follows (working from the bottom up): red cake, orange frosting; yellow cake, green frosting; blue cake, indigo frosting; purple cake.
Frost the top and outside of the cake with white frosting.
Serving Suggestion: Serve with multi-colored cake decorations to create a rainbow effect.
Variation Tip: Nothing; this cake is perfect as it is!
Per Serving: Calories 248; Carbohydrates 40.7g; Protein 2.5g; Fat 10.8g; Sodium 120.4mg; Fiber 0.7g

Shortcake

Prep time: 5 minutes | Cook Time: 10 minutes | Serves: 2

Ingredients:

¼ cup biscuit mix
5 teaspoons milk

Preparation:

1. Combine the biscuit mix and milk in a bowl using a fork. 2. Divide the mixture into two portions. Roll one at a time on a floured surface to fit the Easy-Bake Oven baking pan. Place one portion in the greased baking pan. 3. Bake in the Easy-Bake Oven for about 10 minutes. 4. Allow the shortcake to cool completely. Meanwhile, bake the second portion.
Serving Suggestion: Serve with whipped cream.
Variation Tip: Serve with a fruit filling/fresh fruit of your choice.
Per Serving: Calories 215.3; Carbohydrates 19.4g; Protein 3.7g; Fat 14.7g; Sodium 83.8mg; Fiber 1.1g

Chapter 4 Biscuits and Cookies

Princess Cookies

Prep time: 10 minutes (plus 45 minutes for refrigeration) | Cook Time: 10 minutes | Serves: 4

Ingredients:

2 cups all-purpose flour
1 teaspoon baking powder or baking soda
Pinch of salt
1 cup unsalted butter, softened
1 cup white sugar
2 small eggs
1/3 cup lemon juice
½ teaspoon lemon zest
¼ teaspoon vanilla extract

Preparation:

1. Mix the flour, baking soda, salt, zest, and sugar in a bowl. 2. In a separate bowl, beat the butter with the sugar using an electric hand beater. Then add the eggs. Combine well. 3. Add the vanilla extract and lemon juice. Mix well. 4. Add the flour mixture to the egg mixture. Mix well. 5. Chill the dough for about 45 minutes. 6. Form cookie shapes from the dough and place them onto the prepared baking pan. You'll have to cook in batches. 7. Bake for 10 minutes. 8. Once done, take out and cool on a wire rack.

Serving Suggestion: Serve with milk.

Variation Tip: Use brown sugar instead of white sugar.

Per Serving: Calories 674; Fat 48.9g; Sodium 399mg; Carbs 50g; Fiber 1.8g; Sugar 2.2g; Protein 9.7g

Snow Mound Cookies

Prep time: 10 minutes | Cook Time: 5 minutes | Serves: 2

Ingredients:

6 teaspoons shortening
3 teaspoons icing sugar, plus extra for rolling
1/8 teaspoon vanilla extract
¼ cup flour
Pinch of salt
2 tablespoons walnuts, finely chopped

Preparation:

1. Mix all the ingredients in a bowl. Combine well. 2. Make small ball shapes from the mixture (about 1 inch in size). 3. Place three balls at a time on the prepared baking pan. 4. Flatten them slightly with your hand. 5. Bake for 5 minutes. 6. Bake the next batch. 7. Let the cookies cool completely before rolling in more icing sugar.

Serving Suggestion: Serve the cookies with milk.

Variation Tip: You can use soft butter instead of shortening.

Per Serving: Calories 234; Fat 17.2g; Sodium 78mg; Carbs 16.5g; Fiber 1g; Sugar 3.8g; Protein 3.5g

Potato Drop Cookies

Prep time: 10 minutes | Cook Time: 10 minutes | Serves: 2

Ingredients:

2 tablespoons shortening
2 tablespoons sugar
2 tablespoons brown sugar
1 egg
1⁄8 teaspoon vanilla extract
¼ cup all-purpose flour
1⁄8 teaspoon baking soda
1⁄8 teaspoon salt
¼ cup potato chips, crushed

Preparation:

1. Mix the shortening and sugars in a bowl until fluffy and creamy. 2. Add in the vanilla and the remaining ingredients. Combine well. 3. Drop spoonfuls of the mixture onto the prepared baking pan. 4. Bake for 8–10 minutes. 5. Let the cookies cool completely before serving.
Serving Suggestion: Serve with milk.
Variation Tip: Use white sugar instead of brown sugar.
Per Serving: Calories 416; Fat 24.4g; Sodium 389mg; Carbs 47g; Fiber 1.7g; Sugar 21g; Protein 4.2g

Snowball Cookies

Prep time: 10 minutes | Cook Time: 9 minutes | Serves: 2

Ingredients:

6 teaspoons butter, softened
3 teaspoons powdered sugar, plus extra for rolling
1⁄8 teaspoon vanilla extract
¼ cup flour
Dash of sea salt
4 teaspoons walnuts, chopped

Preparation:

1. Combine all the ingredients in a bowl. 2. Carefully shape the mixture into 1-inch balls and roll them in some powdered sugar. 3. Place the balls in the prepared baking pan and then slightly press down on each of them with your hand. 4. Bake in the oven for 9 minutes. 5. Once done, roll in some more sugar.
Serving Suggestion: Serve with flavored milk.
Variation Tip: None, these cookies are yummy as they are!
Per Serving: Calories 267; Fat 16.2g; Sodium 159mg; Carbs 27.7g; Fiber 1g; Sugar 14.7g; Protein 3.6g

Cream Cheese Snowcaps

Prep time: 20 minutes (plus 2 hours for chilling) | Cook Time: 10 minutes | Serves: 10

Ingredients:

1/3 cup all-purpose flour
½ teaspoon baking powder
2 tablespoons butter or margarine
1 tablespoon cream cheese
2 tablespoons sugar
½ cup powdered sugar, for decoration

Preparation:

1. Combine the flour and baking powder in a bowl. 2. In a separate bowl, beat together the butter and cream cheese until softened. Add the sugar and beat until fluffy. 3. Add the flour mixture and beat until well mixed. 4. Cover and chill for 2 hours or until easy to handle. 5. Shape the dough into 1-inch balls. Place on the prepared baking pan. You'll need to cook in batches. 6. Bake in the Easy-Bake Oven for 12 to 15 minutes or until done. Remove and cool slightly. 7. Pour the powdered sugar into a Ziploc bag. Add a few cookies at a time and shake to cover. 8. Cool the cookies thoroughly and repeat shaking the remaining cookies in sugar.

Serving Suggestion: Serve the cookies with hot chocolate.

Variation Tip: Add some sprinkles and candy on top.

Per Serving: Calories 52; Carbohydrates 6g; Fat 2g; Sodium 26mg; Sugars 4g; Protein 5g; Fiber 0g

Gingersnaps

Prep time: 5 minutes | Cook Time: 10 minutes | Serves: 2

Ingredients:

3 tablespoons butter
¼ cup white sugar
1 tablespoon molasses
½ cup all-purpose flour
¾ teaspoon ground ginger
¼ teaspoon ground cinnamon
½ teaspoon baking soda
⅛ teaspoon salt
2 tablespoons white sugar, for decoration

Preparation:

1. Cream the butter and ¼ cup white sugar until smooth. Gradually beat in the molasses until well blended. 2. Combine the flour, ginger, cinnamon, baking soda, and salt in a bowl. Stir into the molasses mixture to form a dough. 3. Roll the dough into 1-inch balls. Roll the balls in the 2 tablespoons of white sugar. 4. Place the coated cookie balls onto the prepared Easy-Bake Oven baking pan. You'll need to cook in batches. 5. Bake in the Easy-Bake Oven for 8 to 10 minutes. 6. Allow the cookies to cool in the baking pan for 5 minutes before removing them to a wire rack to cool completely.

Serving Suggestion: Serve with milk.

Variation Tip: Add a little cardamom for flavor.

Per Serving: Calories 412; Carbohydrates 64.3g; Protein 16.1g; Fat 10.1g; Sodium 895mg; Fiber 2g

Cranberry Cookies

Prep time: 25 minutes (plus 4 hours for chilling) | Cook Time: 25 minutes | Serves: 16

Ingredients:

¼ cup butter, softened
½ cup packed light brown sugar
½ teaspoon vanilla extract
¼ teaspoon baking soda
¼ teaspoon cream of tartar
¼ teaspoon salt
1¼ cups flour
¼ cup blanched almonds, finely chopped
¼ cup cranberries, coarsely chopped
1 teaspoon lemon rind, grated

For decoration:

Decorating sugar, red and green
Fresh cranberries, halved
Granulated sugar, optional

Preparation:

1. Cream the butter and brown sugar in a small bowl until fluffy. 2. Beat in the vanilla, baking soda, cream of tartar, and salt. 3. Beat in the flour until blended. 4. Stir in the remaining ingredients. Combine well. 5. Divide the batter in half. Wrap each half in clingfilm and chill until firm, about 1 hour. 6. Unwrap and shape each half into an 8-inch-long log. Roll the logs in the colored decorating sugar to coat. Wrap and chill until hard, about 3 hours or overnight. 7. Butter and flour the baking pan. 8. Unwrap one log and slice the dough into ¼-inch-thick rounds. Place two rounds in the pan. Decorate with some more decorating sugar, halved cranberries, and granulated sugar (optional). 9. Bake in the Easy-Bake Oven until beginning to brown around the edges (about 20 minutes). You'll need to bake in batches. The chilled dough can be kept in the refrigerator for up to 4 days and in the freezer for up to 2 months. 10. Cool the pan on a wire rack.

Serving Suggestion: Serve with a milkshake.

Variation Tip: Add the granulated sugar just before baking to give the cookies a crunchy flavor. You can also add some chocolate chips if you like.

Per Serving: Calories 41.9; Carbohydrates 7.6g; Sugars 6.1g; Sodium 0.6mg; Fat 7g; Protein 1g; Fiber 0g

Angel Food Cake Mix Cookies

Prep time: 10 minutes | Cook Time: 20 minutes | Serves: 3

Ingredients:

1 box angel food cake mix
½ cup pineapple soda

Preparation:

1. Using a hand mixer, blend the soda with the angel food cake mix in a bowl. 2. Place heaped tablespoons of the mixture onto the baking pan. Don't put the cookies too close together. You'll need to cook in batches. 3. Bake for 20 minutes or until the tops become light golden brown. 4. Remove and allow them to cool on a wire rack.

Serving Suggestion: Serve with your favorite toppings.

Variation Tip: Use any other flavor of soda you prefer.

Per Serving: Calories 72; Fat 0.2g; Sodium 65mg; Carbs 16.7g| Fiber 0g; Sugar 13.7g; Protein 1g

Sugar Cookies

Prep time: 10 minutes | Cook Time: 10 minutes | Serves: 2

Ingredients:

8 teaspoons butter
4 teaspoons sugar
2 teaspoons brown sugar
Salt
¼ cup flour
1/3 teaspoon baking powder
1/3 teaspoon vanilla extract

Preparation:

1. Mix the butter, salt, and sugar in a bowl. 2. Add the baking powder, flour, and vanilla. 3. Mix well. 4. Form cookie-shaped pieces from the batter and place them on the prepared baking pan. 5. Bake for 10 minutes. 6. Cool and enjoy!

Serving Suggestion: Serve the cookies with milk.

Variation Tip: None, the cookies are simple but delicious!

Per Serving: Calories 238; Fat 15.7g; Sodium 188mg; Carbs 23.4g; Fiber 0.4g; Sugar 11.1g; Protein 1.8g

Almond Cookies

Prep time: 10 minutes | Cook Time: 20 minutes | Serves: 2

Ingredients:

3 tablespoons butter
1½ tablespoons icing sugar
1/8 teaspoon of vanilla
¼ cup almond flour
Pinch of salt
2 tablespoons almonds, chopped

Preparation:

1. Mix the butter, icing sugar, vanilla, almond flour, and salt in a bowl. 2. Blend well, and then add the chopped almonds. Combine well. 3. Shape the mixture into balls and place them on the prepared baking pan. 4. Flatten the balls slightly with your hand. 5. Bake for 5 minutes. 6. Once cool, serve. Enjoy!

Serving Suggestion: Serve with shredded coconut sprinkled on top and a drizzle of melted chocolate.

Variation Tip: Use shortening instead of butter.

Per Serving: Calories 291; Fat 24g; Sodium 78mg; Carbs 16.5g; Fiber 1g; Sugar 3.8g; Protein 3.5g

Rosemary Biscuits

Prep time: 10 minutes | Cook Time: 15 minutes | Serves: 2

Ingredients:

1 can Pillsbury Biscuits
1 sprig rosemary, finely chopped
½ teaspoon salt

Preparation:

1. Lay the biscuits on the prepared baking pan and sprinkle with the rosemary and salt. 2. Bake the biscuits for 13–16 minutes or until their edges are golden.
Serving Suggestion: Serve with cheese.
Variation Tip: You can use dried herbs.
Per Serving: Calories 97; Fat 4.2g; Sodium 897mg; Carbs 12.4g; Fiber 0.4g; Sugar 2.1g; Protein 2.1g

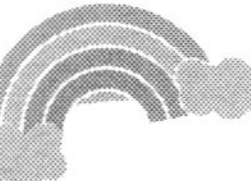

Apple Cookies

Prep time: 4 minutes | Cook Time: 20 minutes | Serves: 2

Ingredients:

¼ cup unsalted butter, softened
½ cup granulated sugar
½ tablespoon apple, grated
1 cup all-purpose flour
⅛ teaspoon salt
⅛ teaspoon baking soda

For the colored sugar:

3 tablespoons granulated sugar
Red food coloring

For the icing:

½ cup powdered sugar
2 tablespoons apple juice

Preparation:

1. In a large bowl, cream the butter and sugar. Add the grated apples; mix well. 2. Sift together the flour, salt, and baking soda; add to the sugar/butter mix. 3. Put the dough onto a floured cutting board, and knead until smooth. 4. Divide the dough in half. Wrap each half separately in plastic wrap and chill until firm, about 1 hour. 5. Shape each half into an 8-inch long log. 6. Mix the 3 tablespoons granulated sugar with 1 to 2 drops of red food coloring. Roll the logs in the colored sugar to coat. Wrap and chill until hard, about 3 hours or overnight. 7. Butter and flour the Easy-Bake Oven baking pan. The dough will be cooked in batches. 8. Unwrap and slice the dough into ¼-inch thick rounds. Place two rounds in the prepared pan, slide into the Easy-Bake Oven, and bake until the cookies begin to brown around the edges, about 20 minutes. 9. Cool the pan on a wire rack. Repeat for the remaining dough. 10. Mix the powdered sugar and apple juice. When the cookies are done, transfer them to wire racks. Brush the cookies with the icing and let them cool.
Serving Suggestion: Serve with cold milk.
Variation Tip: You can add raisins for taste.
Per Serving: Calories 190; Carbohydrates 26g; Protein 4g; Fat 9g; Sodium 105mg; Fiber 3g

Butterscotch Cookies

Prep time: 5 minutes | Cook Time: 10 minutes | Serves: 2

Ingredients:

¼ cup butter or margarine, softened
½ cup packed light brown sugar
1 small egg
½ teaspoon vanilla extract
1 cup all-purpose flour
¼ teaspoon baking soda
¼ cup walnuts, coarsely chopped
1 tablespoon butterscotch chips
Powdered sugar, for decoration

Preparation:

1. In a mixing bowl, cream the butter and brown sugar well. 2. Add the egg and vanilla and beat until smooth and creamy. 3. Mix the flour and baking soda in a separate bowl, then stir into the creamed mixture. 4. Add the walnuts and butterscotch chips, mixing with your hands if necessary. 5. Divide the mixture into two. 6. Wrap each half separately in plastic wrap and chill until firm, about 1 hour. 7. Shape each half into an 8-inch log. 8. Wrap and chill until hard, about 3 hours or overnight. 9. Butter and flour the Easy-Bake Oven baking pan. 10. Unwrap and slice the dough into ¼ -inch thick rounds. Place two rounds into the pan. You'll need to bake the dough in batches. 11. Slide the pan into the Easy-Bake Oven and bake until the cookies begin to brown around the edges, about 20 minutes. 12. Allow the cookies to cool completely on a wire rack, then sprinkle with some powdered sugar.
Serving Suggestion: Serve with milk.
Variation Tip: Nothing; these cookies are delicious as they are!
Per Serving: Calories 199.8; Carbohydrates 25.6g; Protein 3.6g; Fat 2.2g; Sodium 147.6mg; Fiber 4.8g

Chocolate Meringue Cookies

Prep time: 5 minutes | Cook Time: 25 minutes | Serves: 2

Ingredients:

3 egg whites
1 cup granulated sugar
½ teaspoon vinegar
½ teaspoon vanilla extract
2 cups semi-sweet chocolate chips

Preparation:

1. Beat the egg whites until soft peaks form. Keep beating while adding the sugar 1 teaspoon at a time. 2. Add the vanilla and vinegar and keep beating until stiff peaks form. 3. Fold in the chocolate chips. 4. Drop the mixture by teaspoonfuls onto the prepared Easy-Bake Oven baking pan. 5. Bake in the Easy-Bake Oven for about 20-25 minutes or until the cookies appear done.
Serving Suggestion: Serve with warm milk.
Variation Tip: You can make lemon meringue cookies by adding some lemon extract or zest instead of chocolate chips.
Per Serving: Calories 151; Carbohydrates 19.46g; Protein 1.85g; Fat 7.54g; Sodium 95mg; Fiber 0.4g

Candied Cherry Cookies

Prep time: 5 minutes plus 3 hours cooling time | Cook Time: 20 minutes | Serves: 2

Ingredients:

½ cup butter, softened
½ cup brown sugar, packed
½ teaspoon vanilla
1½ cups all-purpose flour
1½ teaspoons baking powder
¼ teaspoon salt
3 tablespoons candied cherries, finely chopped
3 tablespoons almonds, chopped

Preparation:

1. In a bowl, cream the butter with the sugar until light and fluffy. Add the vanilla and mix well. 2. In another bowl, combine the flour, baking powder, and salt. 3. Stir the flour mixture into the butter mixture. Stir in the cherries and nuts. Mix well. 4. Divide the mixture in half. Wrap each half separately in plastic wrap and chill until firm, about 1 hour. 5. Shape each half into an 8-inch log. Wrap and chill until hard, about 3 hours or overnight. 6. Butter and flour the Easy-Bake Oven baking pan. 7. Unwrap and slice the dough into ¼-inch rounds. Place two rounds in the prepared pan. You'll need to bake in batches. 8. Bake in the Easy-Bake Oven until the cookies begin to brown around the edges, about 20 minutes. 9. Cool the cookies on a wire rack.

Serving Suggestion: Serve with cherry jam.

Variation Tip: You can also add some chopped pecans to the mixture.

Per Serving: Calories 197.3; Carbohydrates 21.5g; Protein 2.5g; Fat 11.6g; Sodium 59.8mg; Fiber 1g

Chocolate Chip Cookie Cake

Prep time: 5 minutes | Cook Time: 15 minutes | Serves: 12

Ingredients:

3 teaspoons sugar
1½ teaspoons butter
6 teaspoons flour
⅛ teaspoon baking powder
⅛ teaspoon vanilla extract
12–15 chocolate chips

Preparation:

1. Cream together the sugar and butter in a bowl. 2. Add the flour, baking powder, and vanilla. Combine well. 3. Stir in the milk. Mix well. 4. Add in the chocolate chips. 5. Pour the batter into a prepared Easy-Bake Oven baking pan. 6. Bake for15 minutes in the Easy-Bake Oven. 7. Allow the cake to cool completely before serving.

Serving Suggestion: Serve with milk.

Variation Tip: Use warm milk for a softer texture.

Per Serving: Calories 98; Carbohydrates 7.1g; Protein 1.3g; Fat 6.5g; Sodium 154.6mg; Fiber 0g

Cinnamon Crisps

Prep time: 5 minutes | Cook Time: 10 minutes | Serves: 2

Ingredients:

½ cup flour
¼ teaspoon salt
3 teaspoons shortening
1 tablespoon ice water
Ground cinnamon, for sprinkling
Sugar, for sprinkling
Jam (optional)

Preparation:

1. Combine the flour, salt, and shortening in a bowl with a fork until the mixture resembles peas. 2. Sprinkle with the water and stir gently until the dough forms into a ball. 3. Roll the dough out on a lightly floured surface until about ⅛-inch thick. Sprinkle with some cinnamon and sugar. 4. Cut the dough into desired shapes. Place onto an ungreased Easy-Bake Oven baking pan. You'll need to bake in batches. 5. Bake in the Easy-Bake Oven until the crisps are lightly browned.

Serving Suggestion: Serve with jam on top.

Variation Tip: You can add some chopped apple to the mixture before baking.

Per Serving: Calories 280; Carbohydrates 40g; Protein 4g; Fat 12g; Sodium 200mg; Fiber 1g

Oatmeal Cookies

Prep time: 5 minutes | Cook Time: 10 minutes | Serves: 9

Ingredients:

1½ cups quick-cooking oats
¾ cup all-purpose flour
¼ teaspoon baking soda
¾ cup brown sugar
½ cup shortening
1 tablespoon raisins
1 tablespoon semi-sweet chocolate chips
Butter
Sugar

Preparation:

1. In a medium bowl, combine the oats, flour, baking soda, and brown sugar. Stir to blend well. 2. Cut in the shortening with a pastry blender until the mixture resembles cornmeal. 3. Add in the raisins and chocolate chips. Stir with a spoon until the mixture holds together in one big ball. 4. Arrange the dough, one teaspoonful ball at a time, on the ungreased Easy-Bake Oven baking pan. You may need to cook in batches. 5. Butter the bottom of a small drinking glass. Dip the buttered glass bottom in a small dish of sugar. Flatten each dough ball by pressing it with the sugarcoated glass. 6. Bake for 10 to 12 minutes in Easy-Bake Oven. Remove from the oven and cool the cookies on a wire rack.

Serving Suggestion: Serve with milk.

Variation Tip: Add some chopped nuts for extra crunch and flavor.

Per Serving: Calories 177.6; Carbohydrates 25.5g; Protein 5g; Fat 8.9g; Sodium 286.5mg; Fiber 2.5g

Orange Cookies

Prep time: 5 minutes | Cook Time: 20 minutes | Serves: 7

Ingredients:

¼ cup unsalted butter, softened
½ cup granulated sugar
½ tablespoon orange rind, grated
1 cup all-purpose flour
⅛ teaspoon salt
⅛ teaspoon baking soda

For the colored sugar:

3 tablespoons granulated sugar
Food coloring, yellow and red to make orange

For the icing:

½ cup powdered sugar
2 tablespoons orange juice

Preparation:

1. In a medium bowl, cream the butter and sugar. 2. Add the orange rind and mix well. 3. Add the flour, salt, and baking soda. Combine well. 4. Knead the dough on a floured surface until smooth. 5. Divide the dough in half. Wrap each half separately in plastic wrap and chill until firm. 6. Shape each half into an 8-inch log. 7. Mix the 3 tablespoons of sugar with the yellow and red food coloring to make orange-colored sugar. 8. Roll the logs in the colored sugar to coat. Wrap and chill until hard. 9. Butter and flour the Easy-Bake Oven baking pan. 10. Unwrap and slice the dough into ¼-inch rounds. 11. Place 2 rounds in the prepared pan. You'll need to bake in batches. 12. Bake in the Easy-Bake Oven until the cookies begin to brown around the edges, about 20 minutes. 13. While the cookies are baking, make the icing to add to the still-warm cookies: mix the powdered sugar and orange juice together in a bowl. 14. When the cookies have been transferred to the wire rack, brush them with the icing and then allow them to cool completely.

Serving Suggestion: Serve with a glass of cold milk.

Variation Tip: Use lemon instead.

Per Serving: Calories 155.5; Carbohydrates 24.8g; Protein 3g; Fat 5.4g; Sodium 193.7mg; Fiber 1g

Biscuits Mix

Prep time: 5 minutes | Cook Time: 0 minutes | Serves: 1

Ingredients:

¼ cup baking mix
4 teaspoons milk

Preparation:

1. Combine the baking mix and milk with a fork. 2. Drop ½ teaspoonful onto the prepared baking pan. 3. Indent each teaspoonful by pressing with the back of a spoon or with your fingers. 4. Bake in the Easy-Bake Oven for 10 minutes or until golden brown.

Serving Suggestion: Serve with milk.

Variation Tip: Add a teaspoon of honey for more flavor.

Per Serving: Calories 80; Fat 3g; Carbohydrates 16g; Sugars 2g; Fiber 2g; Protein 3g; Sodium 101mg

Peanut Butter Cookies

Prep time: 5 minutes | Cook Time: 10 minutes | Serves: 12

Ingredients:

2 tablespoons butter
¼ cup cocoa
½ cup sugar
¼ cup milk
Dash of salt
1 teaspoon vanilla extract
1 tablespoon peanut butter
1½ cups oatmeal, uncooked

Preparation:

1. Combine the butter and cocoa in a microwave-safe bowl. Melt the mixture in the microwave. 2. Remove from the microwave. Add the sugar, milk, and salt. 3. Add the vanilla, peanut butter, and oatmeal and thoroughly combine. 4. Form the mixture into 12 cookies. Place them on a prepared Easy-Bake Oven baking pan. You'll need to cook in batches. 5. Bake in the Easy-Bake Oven for 10 minutes. 6. Allow the cookies to cool on a wire rack before serving.

Serving Suggestion: Serve with milk.

Variation Tip: Chopped walnuts can also be used.

Per Serving: Calories 143.8; Carbohydrates 20.3g; Protein 2.6g; Fat 5.8g; Sodium 196.4mg; Fiber 0.5g

Pecan Cookies

Prep time: 5 minutes | Cook Time: 20 minutes | Serves: 12

Ingredients:

1 cup all-purpose flour
Pinch of ground cinnamon
Pinch of salt
8 tablespoons unsalted butter, softened
¼ cup sugar
½ teaspoon vanilla extract
½ cup pecans, coarsely chopped
Powdered sugar, for dusting

Preparation:

1. Cream the sugar, butter, and vanilla together. 2. Add the flour, cinnamon, salt, and pecans. Mix to form a stiff dough. 3. Turn the dough onto a floured surface, then form it into an 8-inch log. Wrap the log in wax paper and refrigerate for 3 or more hours. 4. Unwrap and slice the dough into 3/8-inch rounds. 5. Place 2 rounds onto a prepared Easy-Bake Oven baking pan. You'll need to bake the dough in batches. 6. Bake in the Easy-Bake Oven until the cookies begin to brown at their edges, about 20 minutes. 7. Cool the cookies on a wire rack.

Serving Suggestion: When the cookies are thoroughly cooled, dust them with powdered sugar and serve.

Variation Tip: Chopped walnuts can also be used.

Per Serving: Calories 89.5; Carbohydrates 4.1g; Protein 0.2g; Fat 8.3g; Sodium 50.4mg; Fiber 0.2g

Raisin Chocolate Chip Cookie

Prep time: 5 minutes | Cook Time: 20 minutes | Serves: 9

Ingredients:

1 package cookie mix
2 teaspoons water
1 tablespoon raisins
1 tablespoon mini semi-sweet chocolate chips
Sugar, for sprinkling

Preparation:

1. Combine all the ingredients except for the sugar in a bowl. Stir with a spoon until the mixture holds together in one big ball. 2. Shape one teaspoon of dough at a time into a ball. 3. Arrange the balls on the prepared Easy-Bake Oven baking pan. Press each ball gently with a fork, then lightly sprinkle with sugar. You'll need to cook in batches. 4. Bake for 20 minutes in the Easy-Bake Oven. 5. Allow the cookies to cool on a wire rack.

Serving Suggestion: Serve with milk.

Variation Tip: You can add chopped nuts instead of raisins.

Per Serving: Calories 251.8; Carbohydrates 33.7g; Protein 2.6g; Fat 12.3g; Sodium 185.7mg; Fiber 0.6g

Raisin Cookies

Prep time: 5 minutes | Cook Time: 7 minutes | Serves: 2

Ingredients:

3 teaspoons sugar
1½ teaspoons shortening
6 teaspoons flour
⅛ teaspoon baking powder
⅛ teaspoon vanilla extract
3 teaspoons milk
1 tablespoon raisins

Preparation:

1. Cream the sugar and shortening. 2. Add in the vanilla and milk, mixing well. Add the flour and baking powder, then the raisins. Combine to form a dough. 3. Drop ½ teaspoon of dough onto a greased Easy-Bake Oven baking pan, allowing room for the cookies to spread. You'll need to cook in batches. 4. Bake in the Easy-Bake Oven for 5 to 7 minutes per batch. 5. Allow the cookies to cool on a wire rack.

Serving Suggestion: Serve with milk or tea.

Variation Tip: Add brown sugar for chewiness.

Per Serving: Calories 407.8; Carbohydrates 49.3g; Protein 4.3g; Fat 11.3g; Sodium 484.2mg; Fiber 0.5g

Chapter 5 Desserts and Candies

Fudge Brownies

Prep time: 10 minutes | Cook Time: 15 minutes | Serves: 1

Ingredients:

4 teaspoons flour
4 teaspoons sugar
2 teaspoons cocoa powder
1 tablespoon water
2 teaspoons oil
½ teaspoon vanilla

Preparation:

1. Mix all the ingredients in a bowl. Combine well. 2. Pour the batter into the prepared baking pan. 3. Bake for 15 minutes. 4. Allow to cool, cut into squares and serve.

Serving Suggestion: Serve the brownies with a drizzle of syrup and a scoop of vanilla ice cream.

Variation Tip: Use butter instead of oil.

Per Serving: Calories 192; Fat 9.6g; Sodium 2mg; Carbs 26g; Fiber 1.4g; Sugar 16.4g; Protein 1.7g

Chocolate Milk Brownies

Prep time: 20 minutes | Cook Time: 15 minutes | Serves: 2

Ingredients:

4 tablespoons flour
2 tablespoons milk
4 teaspoons sugar
4 teaspoons chocolate milk mix
2½ teaspoons shortening
2 pinches baking soda
1 dash salt

For the glaze:

6 teaspoons icing sugar
2 teaspoons chocolate milk mix
1 teaspoon milk

Preparation:

1. Mix all the listed ingredients (except the glaze ingredients) together in a bowl until well combined. 2. Pour the batter into the prepared baking pan. 3. Bake for 15 minutes. 4. Meanwhile, mix all the glaze ingredients together in a bowl until smooth. 5. When the brownie is done, let it cool slightly, and then spread the glaze over the top. 6. Let it stand for 2 minutes. 7. Cut into wedges and enjoy.

Serving Suggestion: Serve with ice cream.

Variation Tip: None, this recipe is easy and delicious!

Per Serving: Calories 307; Fat 5.8g; Sodium 311mg; Carbs 61g; Fiber 1.6g; Sugar 47.6g; Protein 2.1g

Baby Brownies

Prep time: 10 minutes | Cook Time: 30 minutes | Serves: 3

Ingredients:

8 ounces semi-sweet chocolate
1/3 cup chocolate syrup
10 tablespoons unsalted butter, at room temperature
1 teaspoon vanilla extract
2 eggs, lightly beaten
¼ cup sugar
Pinch of salt
½ cup all-purpose flour

Preparation:

1. Melt the chocolate in a saucepan over low heat, stirring constantly. 2. Add the syrup and stir until combined. 3. Remove the pan from the heat and add the butter. 4. Beat the mixture until smooth. 5. Add the vanilla and eggs. Mix well. 6. In another mixing bowl, add the flour, sugar, and salt. Mix well to combine. 7. Add the flour mixture to the chocolate mixture. Combine well. 8. Pour the batter into the prepared baking pan. 9. Bake for 30 minutes. 10. Allow the brownies to cool completely before cutting them into 1-inch squares and serving.

Serving Suggestion: Serve the brownies drizzled with chocolate syrup.

Variation Tip: None; the brownies are yummy as they are.

Per Serving: Calories 979; Fat 64g; Sodium 397mg; Carbs 102g; Fiber 6g; Sugar 75g; Protein 10.1g

Banana Split

Prep time: 10 minutes | Cook Time: 20 minutes | Serves: 1

Ingredients:

1 packet sugar cookie dough
2 tablespoons banana, sliced
2 tablespoons strawberries, sliced
2 tablespoons pineapple, drained
2 tablespoons seedless grapes, halved

Preparation:

1. Put the cookie dough in the prepared baking pan and press down. 2. Bake for 20 minutes. 3. Let it cool on a rack, and then place the fruit on top. 4. Refrigerate for2 hours and then serve.

Serving Suggestion: Serve with a whipped cream topping and some toasted almonds.

Variation Tip: Use any kind of fruit you like.

Per Serving: Calories 210; Fat 9.2g; Sodium 101mg; Carbs 32.3g; Fiber 1.2g; Sugar 19.1g; Protein 2.5g

Smores

Prep time: 15 minutes | Cook Time: 25 minutes | Serves: 2

Ingredients:

1 tablespoon mini chocolate chips
2 teaspoons marshmallow cream
2 graham crackers

Preparation:

1. Fill an Easy-Bake Oven-safe cup with the mini chocolate chips. Put the marshmallow cream in another. Cover. 2. Warm in the Easy-Bake oven until melted. Take out and stir. 3. Pour the chocolate onto one graham cracker and the marshmallow onto another. Sandwich them together and enjoy.
Serving Suggestion: Serve with leftover cookies crushed over it.
Variation Tip: You can also top it with a drizzle of hot fudge syrup.
Per Serving: Calories 118; Fat 9g; Sodium 211mg; Carbohydrates 11g; Fiber 3g; Sugars 4g; Protein 2g

Sour Candy Cupcakes

Prep time: 30 minutes | Cook Time: 20 minutes | Serves: 12

Ingredients:

7 ounces lemon cake mix
¼ cup lemon-lime soda
¼ cup lemon juice
2 large eggs, room temperature
1 teaspoon canola oil
½ package (1.5 ounces) orange or lemon gelatin
1 drop lemon oil, optional

Frosting:

1 cup butter, softened
3 cups powdered sugar
½ package (1½ ounces) orange or lemon gelatin
3 tablespoons lemon juice
½ cup orange colored sugar, optional
½ tablespoon citric acid, optional

Preparation:

1. Place cupcake liners on the Easy-Bake Oven baking pan. 2. In a large bowl, combine the cake mix, soda, lemon juice, eggs, canola oil, gelatin, and, if desired, lemon oil. Beat on low speed for 30 seconds and then on medium speed for 2 minutes. 3. Transfer the batter to the cupcake liners. Bake until a toothpick inserted in the center of the cupcakes comes out clean, 18 to 21 minutes. Cool for 10 minutes before removing to a wire rack to cool completely. 4. For the frosting: In a large bowl, combine the butter, powdered sugar, gelatin, and lemon juice; beat until smooth. 5. When the cupcakes have cooled completely, frost them. If desired, in a small bowl, stir together the sugar and citric acid; dip the cupcakes into the sugar mix before frosting. Store in the refrigerator.
Serving Suggestion: Serve with tea.
Variation Tip: Substitute cream for the lemon juice in the frosting.
Per Serving: Calories 382; Carbohydrates 54g; Protein 2g; Fat 19g; Sodium 293mg; Fiber 0g; Sugars 45g

Peanut Butter, Chocolate, & Butterscotch Rice Krispies Treats

Prep time: 15 minutes | Cook Time: 5–7 minutes | Serves: 1

Ingredients:

6 tablespoons Rice Krispies cereal
3 large marshmallows
1 teaspoon peanut butter
1 teaspoon chocolate chips
1 teaspoon butterscotch chips

Preparation:

1. Put the marshmallows and peanut butter in an Easy-Bake Oven-safe cup. Place in the Easy-Bake Oven to melt. 2. In the meantime, place the Rice Krispies into a buttered Easy-Bake Oven pan. 3. Pour the melted marshmallow/peanut butter mixture over the cereal and stir. Press the mixture into the pan. 4. In another cup, add the chocolate chips and butterscotch chips. Put in the Easy-Bake Oven to melt. 5. Pour the chocolate/butterscotch mixture over the cereal mix. Allow it to chill before serving.

Serving Suggestion: Serve with vanilla ice cream.

Variation Tip: You can also top it with mini chocolate chips.

Per Serving: Calories 577.1; Fat 34.5g; Sodium 294.7mg; Carbohydrates 62.5g; Fiber 2.2g; Sugars 47.7g; Protein 9g

Baked Cinnamon Apple Slices

Prep time: 5 minutes | Cook Time: 20 minutes | Serves: 2

Ingredients:

1 large apple
¼ teaspoon butter, melted
⅛ teaspoon ground cinnamon
1 tablespoon sugar

Preparation:

1. Wash the apple and then remove its core. 2. Slice across the apple to make ½-inch thick rings. 3. Grease the Easy-Bake Oven baking pan with butter. Place the apple slices in the pan. 4. Sprinkle the slices lightly with the cinnamon, then the sugar. Top with the butter. 5. Bake in the Easy-Bake Oven for about 20 minutes.

Serving Suggestion: Serve with vanilla ice cream.

Variation Tip: You can use pear slices instead.

Per Serving: Calories 321.2; Carbohydrates 49.3g; Protein 3.4g; Fat 12.73g; Sodium 82mg; Fiber 0.4g

Butterscotch Candy

Prep time: 5 minutes | Cook Time: 10 minutes | Serves: 6

Ingredients:

¼ cup butterscotch chips
2 teaspoons margarine

Preparation:

1. Put the margarine and butterscotch chips into an Easy-Bake Oven-safe cup. 2. Heat up the mixture in the Easy-Bake Oven. 3. Using a spoon, fill candy molds with the melted butterscotch mixture. 4. Place the molds in the refrigerator for 30 minutes or until firm. Remove from the molds.

Serving Suggestion: Serve with a cold glass of milk.

Variation Tip: You can also add some peanuts for taste.

Per Serving: Calories 39.55; Carbohydrates 4.12g; Protein 0.6g; Fat 2.31g; Sodium 114.32mg; Fiber 0.4g

Double Fudge Brownies

Prep time: 5 minutes | Cook Time: 15 minutes | Serves: 3

Ingredients:

2½ tablespoons sugar
1 teaspoon oil
⅛ teaspoon vanilla extract
4 teaspoons chocolate syrup
¼ teaspoon baking cocoa
2½ tablespoons flour

Preparation:

1. Stir together the sugar, oil, vanilla, chocolate syrup, cocoa, and flour until the batter is smooth. 2. Pour the batter into a greased and floured Easy-Bake Oven baking pan. Don't fill past halfway. (You may need to cook in batches.) 3. Bake in the Easy-Bake Oven for 15 minutes. Cool for 5 minutes, then cut and serve.

Serving Suggestion: Serve with vanilla ice cream.

Variation Tip: Add chocolate chips for gooey brownies.

Per Serving: Calories 120; Carbohydrates 16g; Protein 1g; Fat 6g; Sodium 60mg; Fiber 2g

Peanut Butter Candy

Prep time: 5 minutes | Cook Time: 15 minutes | Serves: 5

Ingredients:

¼ cup peanut butter chips

2 teaspoons margarine

Preparation:

1. Put the margarine and chips into an Easy-Bake Oven-proof cup. 2. Heat in the Easy-Bake Oven until melted. 3. Using a spoon, fill candy molds with the melted peanut butter mixture. 4. Place the molds in the refrigerator for 30 minutes or until firm. 5. Remove from the molds and enjoy.

Serving Suggestion: Serve with a milkshake.

Variation Tip: Add chopped peanuts for crunch.

Per Serving: Calories 577; Carbohydrates 73g; Protein 6.6g; Fat 30g; Sodium 415mg; Fiber 1.6g

Cinnamon Bread Pudding

Prep time: 10 minutes | Cook Time: 25 minutes | Serves: 3

Ingredients:

1 egg
½ cup milk
¼ teaspoon vanilla
4 tablespoons sugar
4 slices white bread

For the topping:

Ground cinnamon
1 teaspoon milk
¼ teaspoon butter

Preparation:

1. Break the bread slices into small pieces. 2. Mix the bread pieces with all the other ingredients (not the topping ingredients) together in a bowl. 3. Grease an Easy-Bake Oven baking pan lightly with butter. Fill the pans half full with the mixture and press down. You'll need to bake in batches. 4. Sprinkle lightly with some cinnamon. Add 1 teaspoon of milk and ¼ teaspoon of butter on top of each pudding. 5. Bake in the Easy-Bake Oven for 20 to 25 minutes.

Serving Suggestion: Serve topped with whipped cream and chocolate chips.

Variation Tip: You can add some fresh berries to the batter for flavor.

Per Serving: Calories 181.5; Carbohydrates 23.4g; Protein 5.1g; Fat 3g; Sodium 266 mg; Fiber 0g

Strawberry Cheesecake

Prep time: 5 minutes | Cook Time: 20 minutes | Serves: 2

Ingredients:

1 packet sugar cookie dough

For the cream cheese filling:

2 tablespoons cream cheese

2 teaspoons powdered sugar

2 tablespoons strawberry pie filling

Preparation:

1. Take out the cookie dough and press it evenly into an Easy-Bake Oven baking pan. 2. Bake in the Easy-Bake Oven for 15 to 20 minutes, until golden brown. 3. Cool the cheesecake in the pan on a wire rack. 4. Mix the cream cheese, powdered sugar, and strawberry pie filling to make the cream cheese filling. 5. When the cheesecake has cooled, spread over the cream cheese filling.

Serving Suggestion: Serve topped with whipped cream.

Variation Tip: Add sliced strawberries to the cream cheese filling.

Per Serving: Calories 238.3; Carbohydrates 34.4g; Protein 1.8g; Fat 11.2g; Sodium 87.9mg; Fiber 1g

White Chocolate Candy

Prep time: 5 minutes | Cook Time: 15 minutes | Serves: 6

Ingredients:

¼ cup white chocolate chips

2 teaspoons butter or margarine

Preparation:

1. Put the butter/margarine and chocolate chips into an Easy-Bake Oven-safe cup or pan. Heat in the Easy-Bake Oven. 2. Using a spoon, fill candy molds with the melted white chocolate mixture. 3. Place the molds in the refrigerator for 30 minutes or until firm. 4. Remove from the molds, serve, and enjoy!

Serving Suggestion: Serve as a delicious snack.

Variation Tip: This candy can be made from dark and milk chocolate also.

Per Serving: Calories 201.5; Carbohydrates 25g; Protein 2.8g; Fat 10.2g; Sodium 62.7mg; Fiber 0.4g

Easy Chocolate Candy

Prep time: 15 minutes | Cook Time: 15 minutes | Serves: 6

Ingredients:

¼ cup chocolate chips
Anti-sticking baking spray
2 teaspoons margarine

Preparation:

1. Plug in the easy bake oven, preheating it for 15 minutes. 2. Spritz baking spray on the baking pan. Combine the chocolate chips and margarine in the pan. 3. Bake in the preheated oven for about 10 minutes until melted. 4. Then carefully spoon the melted chocolate chip mixture into the candy molds 5. For around 30 minutes, put the filled molds in the refrigerator. 6. Once the candy is firm, remove it from the molds. 7. Carefully turn the candies onto a platter to serve and enjoy.
Per Serving: Calories 49; Fat 3.3g; Sodium 20mg; Carbs 4.2g; Fiber 0.2g; Sugar 3.6g; Protein 0.6g

Classic S'mores

Prep time: 15 minutes | Cook Time: 6 minutes | Serves: 1

Ingredients:

Anti-sticking baking spray
2 teaspoons marshmallow cream
¼ cup mini chocolate chip
2 graham crackers

Preparation:

1. Plug in the easy bake oven, preheating it for 15 minutes. 2. Spoon marshmallow cream in one warming cup that can fit the oven and place half a cup of small chocolate chips in the other. 3. Set both cups in the baking pan. Bake in the preheated oven for 6 minutes. 4. After cooking time is finished, pour the melted chocolate and the marshmallow onto the graham crackers. 5. Create a sandwich by pressing the two graham crackers together, and enjoy your treat.
Per Serving: Calories 185; Fat 4.9g; Sodium 202mg; Carbs 33.5g; Fiber 0.8g; Sugar 13.4g; Protein 2.4g

Baked Apple Pie

Prep time: 15 minutes | Cook Time: 25 minutes | Serves: 2

Ingredients:

4 teaspoons water
⅓ cup pie crust mix
Anti-sticking baking spray
6 teaspoons apple pie filling

Preparation:

1. Plug in the easy bake oven, preheating it for 15 minutes. 2. Spritz baking spray on the baking pan, followed by dusting with flour. 3. Put pie crust mix and water into medium-sized bowl and whisk to incorporate into a dough. 4. Split the dough into two portions, shaping them into two small balls. 5. Make one of the balls slightly larger than the pan on a floured surface. 6. Place the rolled-out dough into the greased pan, ensuring it fits and covers the bottom and sides. 7. Fill the prepared crust with the apple pie filling. 8. On top of the filled pie, lay down the second ball of dough. 9. Use a fork to seal the edges of the two dough layers together. 10. Lay out the pie onto the baking pan. 11. Bake in the preheated oven for 25 minutes. 12. After cooking time is finished, with pan pusher, shove the baking pan into the "Cooling Chamber". 13. Give it about five minutes to cool down. 14. Carefully turn the apple pie onto a platter to serve.

Per Serving: Calories 43; Fat 1.5g; Sodium 45mg; Carbs 7.3g; Fiber 0.2g; Sugar 2.6g; Protein 0.4g

White Chocolate Peanut Butter Bird Nest

Prep time: 15 minutes | Cook Time: 6 minutes | Serves: 4

Ingredients:

1 bag chow mein noodles
1 bag M&Ms
½ bag white chocolate chips
2 tablespoons peanut butter

Preparation:

1. Plug in the easy bake oven, preheating it for 15 minutes. 2. Fill a cake pan that fits the oven with white chocolate chips. 3. Set the cake pan in the baking pan. 4. Bake in the preheated oven for 6 minutes.5. After cooking time is finished, with pan pusher, shove the baking pan into the "Cooling Chamber". 6. Give it about five minutes to cool down. 7. In a small bowl, drizzle melted white chocolate over the chow mein noodles and gently mix them together. 8. Quickly shape nests on waxed paper using approximately 2 tablespoons of the mixture for each nest. 9. Make sure to work swiftly so the chocolate doesn't have time to harden. 10. Place a few small dots of peanut butter inside each nest to assist in adhering the jelly beans. 11. Add M&M "eggs" to complete the nests.

Per Serving: Calories 280; Fat 16.9g; Sodium 113mg; Carbs 29.2g; Fiber 1.3g; Sugar 21g; Protein 4.7g

Butter Cinnamon Crisps

Prep time: 15 minutes | Cook Time: 15 minutes | Serves: 8

Ingredients:

1 cup sugar
Anti-sticking baking spray
1 stick butter, melted
1 tablespoon ground cinnamon
3 whole flour tortillas

Preparation:

1. Plug in the easy bake oven, preheating it for 15 minutes. 2. Spritz baking spray on the baking pan, followed by dusting with flour. 3. Merge the sugar and cinnamon in a mixing bowl. 4. Apply butter on one side of the flour tortillas. 5. Dust a generous amount of the cinnamon sugar mixture over it. 6. Flip the tortillas to the other side and repeat the process by sprinkling more of the cinnamon sugar mixture on that side as well. 7. Lay out the tortillas onto the baking pan about 1½-inch apart. 8. Bake in the preheated oven for 15 minutes. 9. After cooking time is finished, with pan pusher, shove the baking pan into the "Cooling Chamber". 10. Give it about five minutes to cool down. 11. Break into pieces and serve.

Per Serving: Calories 246; Fat 12.6g; Sodium 183mg; Carbs 34.3g; Fiber 2g; Sugar 25g; Protein 1.7g

Cinnamon–Butter Apple Slices

Prep time: 15 minutes | Cook Time: 20 minutes | Serves: 6

Ingredients:

⅛ teaspoon cinnamon
Anti-sticking baking spray
1 large apple
¼ teaspoon butter
1 tablespoon sugar

Preparation:

1. Plug in the easy bake oven, preheating it for 15 minutes. 2. Spritz baking spray on the baking pan, followed by dusting with flour. 3. Start by washing a large apple and removing the core from the center. 4. Slice the apple horizontally to create rings that are about ½ inch thick. 5. Lay the apple slices onto the baking pan. 6. Lightly sprinkle the apple slices with cinnamon and sugar. 7. Place small pieces of butter on top of the apple slices. 8. Bake in the preheated oven for 20 minutes. 9. After cooking time is finished, with pan pusher, shove the baking pan into the "Cooling Chamber". 10. Give it about five minutes to cool down. 11. Carefully turn the baked apples onto a platter to serve and enjoy.

Per Serving: Calories 28; Fat 0.2 g; Sodium 1mg; Carbs 7.2g; Fiber 0.9g; Sugar 5.9g; Protein 0.1g

Butterscotch Hard Candy

Prep time: 15 minutes | Cook Time: 15 minutes | Serves: 6

Ingredients:

2 teaspoons margarine

¼ cup butterscotch morsels

Preparation:

1. Throw butterscotch morsels and margarine in a melting pan, and then set it in the baking pan of easy bake oven. 2. Bake in the preheated oven for 15 minutes. 3. Then stir until well combined and carefully spoon the melted chocolate chip mixture into the candy molds 4. For around 30 minutes, put the filled molds in the refrigerator. 5. Once the candy is firm, remove it from the molds. 6. Carefully turn the candies onto a platter to serve and enjoy.

Per Serving: Calories 58; Fat 3.9g; Sodium 21mg; Carbs 6g; Fiber 0g; Sugar 6g; Protein 0g

Butter Cinnamon Bread Pudding

Prep time: 15 minutes | Cook Time: 12 minutes | Serves: 8

Ingredients:

¼ teaspoon vanilla
4 tablespoons sugar
Anti-sticking baking spray
1 egg
½ cup milk
4 slices white bread, cut into small pieces
Topping
1 teaspoon milk
Cinnamon
¼ teaspoon butter

Preparation:

1. Plug in the easy bake oven, preheating it for 15 minutes. 2. Spritz baking spray on the baking pan, followed by dusting with flour. 3. Merge all the ingredients except the toppings into a medium-sized bowl and whisk to incorporate well. 4. Fill the pans halfway and press the contents down. 5. Lightly sprinkle cinnamon on top. 6. Add 1 teaspoon of milk and ¼ teaspoon of butter on top of each pudding. 7. Bake in the preheated oven for 12 minutes. 8. After cooking time is finished, with pan pusher, shove the baking pan into the "Cooling Chamber". 9. Give it about five minutes to cool down. 10. Carefully turn the bread pudding onto a platter to serve and enjoy.

Per Serving: Calories 52; Fat 1.1g; Sodium 46mg; Carbs 9.2g; Fiber 0.2g; Sugar 6.9g; Protein 1.5g

Cheesy Apple Rings

Prep time: 15 minutes | Cook Time: 15 minutes | Serves: 6

Ingredients:

Anti-sticking baking spray
2 tablespoons cheddar cheese, shredded
1 large apple

Preparation:

1. Plug in the easy bake oven, preheating it for 15 minutes. 2. Spritz baking spray on the baking pan, followed by dusting with flour. 3. Start by washing a large apple and removing the core from the center. 4. Slice the apple horizontally to create rings that are about ½ inch thick. 5. Lay the apple slices onto the baking pan. 6. Top the apple slices with cheese. 7. Bake in the preheated oven for 15 minutes. 8. After cooking time is finished, with pan pusher, shove the baking pan into the "Cooling Chamber". 9. Give it about five minutes to cool down. 10. Carefully turn the baked apples onto a platter to serve and enjoy.

Per Serving: Calories 29; Fat 0.9g; Sodium 15mg; Carbs 5.2g; Fiber 0.9g; Sugar 3.9g; Protein 0.7g

Banana Strawberry S'mores

Prep time: 15 minutes | Cook Time: 8 minutes | Serves: 1

Ingredients:

Anti-sticking baking spray
1 tablespoon mini chocolate chips
2 graham crackers
Banana slices
2 teaspoons marshmallow cream
Strawberry slices

Preparation:

1. Plug in the easy bake oven, preheating it for 15 minutes. 2. Spoon marshmallow cream in one warming cup that fits the oven and half a cup of mini chocolate chips in the other. 3. Set both cups in the baking pan. 4. Bake in the preheated oven for 8 minutes. 5. Arrange banana and strawberry slices on top of one graham cracker. 6. Pour the melted chocolate over the fruit and add marshmallow on top of the chocolate. 7. Top with another graham cracker to create a sandwich, and enjoy your treat.

Per Serving: Calories 246; Fat 6g; Sodium 255mg; Carbs 46.4g; Fiber 1.6g; Sugar 21.5g; Protein 2.3g

Homemade Blueberry Pie

Prep time: 15 minutes | Cook Time: 25 minutes | Serves: 6

Ingredients:

4 teaspoons water
⅓ cup pie crust mix
Anti-sticking baking spray
6 teaspoons blueberry pie filling

Preparation:

1. Plug in the easy bake oven, preheating it for 15 minutes. 2. Spritz baking spray on the baking pan, followed by dusting with flour. 3. Put pie crust mix and water into medium-sized bowl and whisk to incorporate into a dough. 4. Split the dough into two portions, shaping them into two small balls. 5. Make one of the balls slightly larger than the pan on a floured surface. 6. Place the rolled-out dough into the greased pan, ensuring it fits and covers the bottom and sides. 7. Fill the prepared crust with the blueberry pie filling. 8. On top of the filled pie, lay down the second ball of dough. 9. Use a fork to seal the edges of the two dough layers together. 10. Lay out the pie onto the baking pan. 11. Bake in the preheated oven for 25 minutes. 12. After cooking time is finished, with pan pusher, shove the baking pan into the "Cooling Chamber". 13. Give it about five minutes to cool down. 14. Carefully turn the blueberry pie onto a platter to serve.

Per Serving: Calories 16; Fat 0.5g; Sodium 13mg; Carbs 2.7g; Fiber 0.1g; Sugar 1.3g; Protein 0.1g

Chapter 6 Main Dishes

Sweet Mini Pizzas

Prep time: 10 minutes | Cook Time: 15 minutes | Serves: 1

Ingredients:

For the cookie dough:
7 teaspoons shortening
7 teaspoons sugar
Pinch of salt
¼ cup flour
1/8 teaspoon baking powder
1/8 teaspoon vanilla extract

For the cream cheese topping:
¼ cup cream cheese, at room temperature
¼ cup sugar
¼ teaspoon vanilla extract

For the topping:
2 tablespoons banana, sliced
2 tablespoons strawberry, sliced
2 tablespoons apple, sliced
2 tablespoons blueberries
3 tablespoons mini chocolate chips

Preparation:

Cookie dough: 1. Cream together the butter, sugar, and salt. Add the flour, baking powder, and vanilla. 2. Mix until a dough-like consistency is formed. 3. Sprinkle 1 teaspoon of flour on the (clean!) countertop. Roll out the cookie dough and use a knife to cut it into 1-inch circles. 4. Place the circles onto the greased Easy-Bake Oven baking pan. 5. Bake for 5 minutes. 6. Remove from the oven when done and allow to cool.
Cream cheese topping: 1. Mix together the sugar, vanilla, and softened cream cheese until smooth. 2. Evenly spread over the cooled pizzas.
Topping: Add the sliced fruit and mini chocolate chips. Enjoy!
Serving Suggestion: Serve with a chocolate dipping sauce.
Variation Tip: You can add any other fruit of your choice for the topping.
Per Serving: Calories 282; Fat 10.2g; Sodium 1017.4mg; Carbohydrates 24.5g; Fiber 2.5g; Sugars 2.7g; Protein 23.2g

Cheese and Pepperoni Muffins

Prep time: 10 minutes | Cook Time: 20 minutes | Serves: 6

Ingredients:

1 English muffin, split
2 tablespoons spaghetti sauce
¼ cup mozzarella cheese, shredded

Toppings:

1 tablespoon pepperoni, diced
1 tablespoon mushroom, diced
1 tablespoon onion, diced

Preparation:

1. Place each half of the muffin in the prepared baking pan. 2. Add the spaghetti sauce and then the toppings on top of each half. 3. Top each half with the cheese. 4. Bake for 15–20 minutes. 5. Enjoy!

Serving Suggestion: Serve with milk.

Variation Tip: Use your favorite type of cheese.

Per Serving: Calories 290; Fat 12.3g; Sodium 695mg; Carbs 35.5g; Fiber 1.2g; Sugar 2.1g; Protein 11.7g

Easy-Bake Oven Pizza

Prep time: 10 minutes | Cook Time: 20 minutes | Serves: 4

Ingredients:

2 tablespoons all-purpose flour
1/8 teaspoon baking powder
Dash of salt
1 teaspoon margarine
2¼ teaspoons milk
1 tablespoon pizza sauce
1½ tablespoons mozzarella cheese, shredded

Preparation:

1. Stir together the flour, baking powder, salt, and margarine until a crumbly dough is formed. Slowly add the milk while stirring constantly. 2. Shape the dough into a ball and place it into the greased baking pan. Use your fingers to pat the dough evenly over the bottom of the pan, then up the sides. 3. Pour the sauce evenly over the dough, then sprinkle with the cheese. Bake for 20 minutes.

Serving Suggestion: Serve with a green salad.

Variation Tip: Add mushrooms and olives to give the pizza some extra flavor.

Per Serving: Calories 142; Carbohydrates 14 g; Protein 5g; Fat 7g; Sodium 1102 mg; Fiber 3g; Sugar 0g

Beef and Tater Tot Casserole

Prep time: 10 minutes | Cook Time: 30 minutes | Serves: 1

Ingredients:

½ onion, diced
½ pound ground beef
5 ounces cream of broccoli soup
2 ounces cheese soup
4 ounces cream of mushroom soup
Pinch of garlic powder
Pinch of Italian seasoning
½ cup frozen vegetables, diced
1/3 cup cheddar cheese, shredded, plus more
Salt and freshly ground black pepper, to taste
Tater tots, as needed
1 teaspoon butter

Preparation:

1. Heat the butter in a saucepan. Add the onions and cook for 5 minutes. 2. Add the ground beef and cook for 10 minutes. 3. Mix the soups, vegetables, garlic powder, Italian seasoning, cheese, black pepper, and salt in a saucepan. 4. Add the ground beef and onion to the soup mixture. Mix well. 5. Carefully place some of the mixture into the baking pan. Be careful not to overfill. Place the remaining mixture into an airtight container and refrigerate to use later. It will keep for up to 5 days (longer if frozen). 6. Put some tater tots on top and sprinkle with more cheese. 7. Bake for 30 minutes. 8. Serve and enjoy.

Serving Suggestion: Serve it hot.
Variation Tip: None; this recipe is delicious as it is.
Per Serving: Calories 1028; Fat 48.2g; Sodium 1775mg; Carbs 77.9g; Fiber 9.3g; Sugar 4.7g; Protein 69.5g

Banana Split Pizza

Prep time: 20 minutes | Cook Time: 20 minutes | Serves: 1

Ingredients:

1 package sugar cookie dough
Whipped cream
2 tablespoons banana, sliced
2 tablespoons strawberries, sliced
2 tablespoons canned crushed pineapple, drained
2 tablespoons seedless grapes, halved

Preparation:

1. Press the cookie dough evenly into the Easy-Bake Oven baking pan. 2. Bake in the Easy-Bake Oven for 15 to 20 minutes, until golden brown. Cool in the pan on a wire rack. 3. Spread the whipped topping over the cooled crust. Arrange the fruit in a decorative pattern.

Serving Suggestion: Serve as a snack or dessert.
Variation Tip: Sprinkle some cinnamon powder on top.
Per Serving: Calories 225; Carbohydrates 17g; Protein 2g; Fat 15g; Sodium 282mg; Fiber 1g; Sugar 2g

English Muffin Pizza

Prep time: 30 minutes | Cook Time: 15–20 minutes | Serves: 1

Ingredients:

1 English muffin, split
2 tablespoons ready-made spaghetti sauce
Mozzarella cheese, shredded

For the topping:

½ pepperoni, sliced
1 tablespoon ground meat sausage, sliced
1 mushroom, sliced
½ bell pepper, sliced
½ onion, sliced

Preparation:

1. Place each half of the English muffin in the baking pan. 2. Top each half with about 1 tablespoon of prepared sauce. Top with the additional pre-cooked toppings. Top with the shredded cheese. 3. Bake in the Easy-Bake Oven for about 15–20 minutes.

Serving Suggestion: Serve with fresh basil on top.

Variation Tip: You can also add some black olives.

Per Serving: Calories 152.75; Fat 11.87g; Sodium 638.38mg; Carbohydrates 4.26g; Sugars 3.13g; Fiber 0.95g; Protein 7.67g

Cheesy Potato Hot Dogs

Prep time: 5 minutes | Cook Time: 15 minutes | Serves: 2

Ingredients:

2 hot dogs
½ cup mashed potato
½ cup cheddar or parmesan cheese, grated

Preparation:

1. Slice the hot dogs into thirds. Cut a slit in the hot dogs lengthwise. Place in the Easy-Bake Oven baking pan. 2. Fill the hot dog openings with mashed potatoes. Sprinkle the tops with cheese. 3. Bake in the Easy-Bake Oven for about 15 minutes or until heated through and slightly browned on top.

Serving Suggestion: Serve with dill garnishing or enjoy as it is.

Variation Tip: Add mustard sauce to the hot dog for tanginess.

Per Serving: Calories 197.3; Carbohydrates 21.5g; Protein 2.5g; Fat 11.6g; Sodium 59.8mg; Fiber 1g

Prep time: 15 minutes | Cook Time: 20 minutes | Serves: 2

Ingredients:

3 tablespoons all-purpose flour
1/6 tcaspoon baking powdcr
Pinch of salt
1 teaspoon butter
2½ teaspoons milk
1 tablespoon pizza sauce
1½ tablespoons mozzarella cheese, shredded

Preparation:

1. Mix the baking powder, flour, salt, and butter in a bowl. 2. Add the milk and keep stirring. 3. Combine the mixture into a dough and place it in the prepared baking pan. 4. Use clean fingers to pat the dough over the bottom of the pan, then pat it up the sides. 5. Pour the pizza sauce evenly over the dough. 6. Sprinkle with the mozzarella cheese. 7. Bake for 20 minutes. 8. Serve.

Serving Suggestion: Serve with chopped fresh basil on top.

Variation Tip: Use parmesan cheese instead of mozzarella cheese.

Per Serving: Calories 127; Fat 6g; Sodium 251mg; Carbs 11.1g; Fiber 0.5g; Sugar 0.6g; Protein 7.6g

Lasagna

Prep time: 5 minutes | Cook Time: 15 minutes | Serves: 2

Ingredients:

4 ounces cooked lasagna sheets
1 cube ricotta cheese, shredded
½ cup mozzarella cheese, shredded
1 egg
Spaghetti sauce

Preparation:

1. Pour enough spaghetti sauce into an Easy-Bake Oven baking pan to cover the bottom (about ¼ -inch thick). 2. Mix the cheeses and egg in a bowl. 3. Lay a lasagna sheet on a flat surface. Using a spatula, spread some of the cheese mixture over the top of the sheet. Leave enough room at either end and along the sides so the mixture won't ooze out when you roll the sheet up. 4. Roll the sheet up and place it in the Easy-Bake Oven pan. 5. Repeat steps 3 and 4 for the remaining lasagna sheets and cheese mixture. 6. Pour spaghetti sauce on top of the rolled-up pasta. 7. Bake in the Easy-Bake Oven for about 15 minutes.

Serving Suggestion: Serve warm with a side salad.

Variation Tip: Add some cooked beef mince for extra flavor.

Per Serving: Calories 248; Carbohydrates 40.7g; Protein 2.5g; Fat 10.8g; Sodium 120.4mg; Fiber 0.7g

Prep time: 10 minutes | Cook Time: 5 minutes | Serves: 1

Ingredients:

2 slices deli ham
1 bagel, cut in half, toasted
6 tablespoons processed cheese, softened

Preparation:

1. Put one ham slice on top of a bagel half. 2. Put two tablespoons of cheese in an oven-safe cup and cook it for 3 to 4 minutes to get a smooth texture. 3. Drizzle the warm cheese on top of the ham. 4. Cover the bagel with another half. 5. Enjoy.
Serving Suggestion: Serve with milk.
Variation Tip: Use your favorite kind of cheese.
Per Serving: Calories 477; Fat 23.7g; Sodium 2187mg; Carbs 40g; Fiber 2g; Sugar 8.8g; Protein 30g

Ham And Spinach Quiche

Prep time: 35 minutes | Cook Time: 30 minutes | Serves: 2

Ingredients:

1⅓ cups all-purpose flour, sifted
¼ teaspoon salt
4 tablespoons cold unsalted butter, cubed
¼ cup cold vegetable shortening, cubed
4½ tablespoons ice-cold water

For the filling:

2 eggs
¼ cup cream
⅛ cup ham, diced
¼ cup cheese, grated
¼ cup spinach, chopped
Salt and ground black pepper, to taste

Preparation:

1. In a medium bowl, stir together the flour and the salt. Using a pastry cutter or two knives, cut in the butter and shortening until the mixture resembles coarse crumbles. 2. Sprinkle the water, 1 tablespoon at a time, over the flour mixture and toss together with a fork until a dough starts to form. The dough should be slightly sticky or tacky. 3. Form the dough into a disc shape, wrap it in plastic wrap, and chill it in the refrigerator for at least 30 minutes before using. 4. Put all the filling ingredients in a medium mixing bowl. Stir together until thoroughly combined. 5. On a lightly floured surface, roll out the dough to ⅛-inch thickness. Use the Easy-Bake Oven baking pan to cut out one layer of dough per quiche. 6. Spray the pan with a generous amount of vegetable cooking spray, and then press the dough into the bottom and up the sides of the pan. Place two to three tablespoons of the filling in the center of the quiche. 7. Place the baking pan in the Easy-Bake Oven and bake for 30 minutes.
Serving Suggestion: Serve warm with a side salad and enjoy.
Variation Tip: You can also add some chopped bell pepper to the filling.
Per Serving: Calories 215.3; Carbohydrates 19.4g; Protein 3.7g; Fat 14.7g; Sodium 83.8mg; Fiber 1.1g

Quesadillas

Prep time: 5 minutes | Cook Time: 10 minutes | Serves: 2

Ingredients:

1 teaspoon butter or margarine
2 flour or corn tortillas
Cheddar/Jack cheese, grated

Preparation:

1. Melt the butter/margarine in the microwave. Brush one side of a tortilla with half the melted butter. Turn the tortilla over. 2. Top with the grated cheese, and place the other tortilla on top, creating a cheese sandwich. 3. Brush the remaining melted butter on top of the tortilla. 4. Cut the tortilla into quarters place one quarter in the Easy-Bake Oven baking pan. 5. Bake in the Easy-Bake Oven (one quarter at a time) until the cheese is melted and the top is brown. 6. To add a little spice to your quesadillas, add olives, salsa, chopped cooked chicken pieces, or other chopped veggies before adding the cheese.

Serving Suggestion: Serve topped with more grated cheese.
Variation Tip: Add mozzarella for extra flavor.
Per Serving: Calories 270; Carbohydrates 38g; Protein 3g; Fat 12g; Sodium 250mg; Fiber 1g

Deep Dish Pizza

Prep time: 5 minutes | Cook Time: 20 minutes | Serves: 1

Ingredients:

2 tablespoons all-purpose flour
⅛ teaspoon baking powder
Dash of salt
1 teaspoon margarine
2¼ teaspoons milk
1 tablespoon pizza sauce
1½ tablespoons mozzarella cheese, shredded

Preparation:

1. Stir together the flour, baking powder, salt, and margarine until the dough looks like medium-sized crumbs. Slowly add the milk while stirring. 2. Shape the dough into a ball and place it into the greased Easy-Bake Oven baking pan. Use your fingers to pat the dough evenly over the bottom of the pan, then up the sides. 3. Pour the sauce evenly over the dough, and then sprinkle with the cheese. 4. Bake for 20 minutes in the Easy-Bake Oven.

Serving Suggestion: Serve warm topped with extra cheese topping.
Variation Tip: Add cooked chicken chunks and extra cheese for flavor.
Per Serving: Calories 190; Carbohydrates 26g; Protein 4g; Fat 9g; Sodium 105mg; Fiber 3g

Ranch Chicken Pizza

Prep time: 5 minutes | Cook Time: 20 minutes | Serves: 2

Ingredients:

2 tablespoons all-purpose flour
1/8 shredded teaspoon baking powder
Dash of salt
1 tablespoon margarine
2¼ teaspoons milk
2 tablespoons cooked chicken, chopped
1 tablespoon ranch salad dressing
2 tablespoons mozzarella cheese, shredded
2 tablespoons cheddar cheese, shredded
1 tablespoon tomatoes, chopped
1 teaspoon green onions, chopped

Preparation:

1. Stir together the flour, baking powder, salt, and margarine in a bowl until the dough resembles medium-sized crumbs. Slowly add the milk while stirring. 2. Shape the dough into a ball 3. Place the dough ball on a greased Easy-Bake Oven baking pan. 4. Use your fingers to pat the dough evenly over the bottom of the pan and up the sides. 5. Pour the ranch dressing evenly over the dough. Add the chicken pieces. 6. Top with the tomatoes and green onions. Sprinkle with the cheese. 7. Bake in the Easy-Bake Oven for 20 minutes.

Serving Suggestion: Serve with tomato ketchup.

Variation Tip: Use sliced olives and mushrooms for extra flavor.

Per Serving: Calories 321.2; Carbohydrates 49.3g; Protein 3.4g; Fat 12.73g; Sodium 82mg; Fiber 0.4g

Barbeque Chicken Pizza

Prep time: 5 minutes | Cook Time: 20 minutes | Serves: 2

Ingredients:

2 tablespoons all-purpose flour
1/8 shredded teaspoon baking powder
Dash of salt
1 teaspoon margarine
2¼ teaspoons milk
2 tablespoons cooked chicken, chopped
1 tablespoon barbecue sauce, any brand
1½ tablespoons mozzarella cheese, shredded

Preparation:

1. Stir together the flour, baking powder, salt, and margarine in a bowl until the dough looks like medium-sized crumbs. Slowly add the milk while stirring. 2. Shape the dough into a ball and place it into a greased Easy-Bake Oven baking pan. Use your fingers to pat the dough evenly over the bottom of the pan, then up the sides. 3. Pour barbecue sauce evenly over the dough. Add the chicken pieces. Sprinkle with the cheese. 4. Bake in the Easy-Bake Oven for 20 minutes.

Serving Suggestion: Serve with your favorite sauce.

Variation Tip: You can use sliced olives and mushrooms for taste.

Per Serving: Calories 424; Carbohydrates 57.7g; Protein 3.8g; Fat 22g; Sodium 379mg; Fiber 2.4g

Dessert Pizza

Prep time: 5 minutes | Cook Time: 5 minutes | Serves: 2

Ingredients:

Cookie Dough:

7 teaspoons shortening
7 teaspoons sugar
Pinch of salt
¼ cup flour
⅛ teaspoon baking powder
⅛ teaspoon vanilla extract

For the cream cheese topping:

¼ cup cream cheese (at room temperature)
¼ cup sugar
¼ teaspoon vanilla extract

Toppings:

½ banana, sliced
4 strawberries, sliced
¼ apple, sliced
8 blueberries
2 tablespoons mini chocolate chips

Preparation:

1. Cream together the butter, sugar, and salt. 2. Add the flour, baking powder, and vanilla. Combine well. 3. Mix until a ball of dough forms. 4. Sprinkle 1 teaspoon of flour on a countertop. Roll out the dough and use a knife to cut it into 1-inch circles. 5. Place the circles onto a greased Easy-Bake Oven baking pan. You'll need to cook in batches. 6. Bake the mini pizzas for 5 minutes each batch. 7. Allow the pizzas to cool. 8. For the cream cheese topping: Mix together the sugar, vanilla, and softened cream cheese until smooth. Spread the topping over the top of each cooled pizza. 9. Add the sliced fruit and mini chocolate chips over the top of the cream cheese topping. Serve and enjoy!

Serving Suggestion: Serve with whipped cream. You can also add mini marshmallows and chocolate syrup.

Variation Tip: Add dried fruits for some crunch.

Per Serving: Calories 238.3; Carbohydrates 34.4g; Protein 1.8g; Fat 11.2g; Sodium 87.9mg; Fiber 1g

Cheese Quesadilla

Prep time: 5 minutes | Cook Time: 5 minutes | Serves: 1

Ingredients:

1 small tortilla
1 cup cheddar cheese, shredded

Preparation:

1. Cut the tortilla into wedges small enough to fit inside the baking pan. 2. Sandwich the cheese between two wedges. 3. Bake for 5 minutes or until the cheese melts. 4. Once done, serve.

Serving Suggestion: Serve with your favorite toppings.

Variation Tip: Use mozzarella cheese instead.

Per Serving: Calories 508; Fat 38.1g |Sodium 713mg; Carbs 12.2g; Fiber 1.5g; Sugar 0.8g; Protein 29.5g

Chapter 7 Pies And Tarts

Ambrosia Cream Pie

Prep time: 20 minutes | Cook Time: 10 minutes | Serves: 1

Ingredients:

1 package pie-crust dough
1 serving vanilla pudding
Whipped cream, for decoration
Candied cherries, for decoration
Pineapple slices, for dccoration

Preparation:

To the crust: 1. Allow the pie-crust dough to reach room temperature, then unroll it onto a floured surface. 2. Cut a piece out of the dough, slightly larger than the Easy-Bake Oven baking pan. 3. Place the round of dough into the pan, pushing the edges up against the sides. 4. Bake for 10 minutes in the Easy-Bake Oven. 5. Remove, let it cool, and remove it from the tin. (It should come out easily.)
To make the filling: 1. Place a layer of vanilla pudding in the bottom of the cooked crust. Put the cherries and pineapple on top of the pudding. 2. Spread a generous layer of whipped cream on top of the fruit. 3. Decorate with a few more slices of pineapple and cherry.
Serving Suggestion: Serve the pie with vanilla ice cream.
Variation Tip: You can also use sliced strawberries or bananas.
Per Serving: Calories 69; Fat 1.6g; Sodium 112.5mg; Carbohydrates 4.5g; Fiber 18g; Sugars 2.1g; Protein 9.2g

Oreo Butterscotch Pie

Prep time: 7 minutes | Cook Time: 10 minutes | Serves: 1

Ingredients:

1⁄3 cup Oreo cookie crumbs
1 teaspoon cocoa powder
1 tablespoon sweetened condensed milk
1⁄8 teaspoon milk
2 tablespoons butterscotch chips, divided

Preparation:

1. Combine all the ingredients in a bowl except for 1 tablespoon of butterscotch chips and 1 teaspoon of cookie crumbs. Mix thoroughly. 2. Spread the mixture into the Easy-Bake Oven baking pan and bake for about 10 minutes. 3. When the baking time is over, take the pie out and allow it to cool. 4. Add the remaining cookie crumbs and butterscotch chips on top.
Serving Suggestion: Serve the pie with ice cream or whipped cream.
Variation Tip: You can use meringue as a topping for the pie.
Per Serving: Calories 181; Fat 15.5g; Sodium 19mg; Carbohydrates 2.3g; Fiber 2.2g; Sugars 1.3g; Protein 8.4g

Lemon Whipped Cream Pie

Prep time: 5 minutes | Cook Time: 17 minutes | Serves: 2

Ingredients:

3 tablespoons sweetened condensed milk
1 teaspoon egg yolk
2 teaspoons lemon juice
⅛ teaspoon lemon rind, grated
1 packet sugar cookie dough
Whipped cream, for serving

Preparation:

1. Butter the Easy-Bake Oven baking pan. 2. Take out the sugar cookie dough and press it into the bottom of the pan and up the sides. 3. Bake in the Easy-Bake Oven for 5 minutes. 4. While it's baking, mix together the egg yolk, lemon juice, condensed milk, and grated lemon rind. 5. Remove the baked crust from the oven. Pour the lemon mixture over the crust while it's still warm. 6. Bake in the Easy-Bake Oven for 12 minutes. Allow the pie to cool completely in the pan.
Serving Suggestion: Add whipped cream on top and serve.
Variation Tip: You can use orange instead of lemon.
Per Serving: Calories 280; Carbohydrates 40g; Protein 4g; Fat 12g; Sodium 200mg; Fiber 1g

Strawberry Pie

Prep time: 5 minutes | Cook Time: 30 minutes | Serves: 2

Ingredients:

⅓ cup pie crust mix
4 teaspoons water
2 tablespoons strawberry pie filling

Preparation:

1. In a small bowl, combine the pie crust mix and water with a fork. Stir the mixture gently to form a ball. 2. Divide the dough in half, forming 2 small balls. 3. On a floured board, roll out one ball slightly larger than the Easy-Bake Oven baking pan. Fit it into the greased pan. 4. Fill it with the pie filling. 5. Roll out the second ball of dough and place it on top. Seal the edges with a fork. 6. Bake in the Easy-Bake Oven for 25 to 30 minutes.
Serving Suggestion: Serve with whipped cream on top.
Variation Tip: Top with some fresh sliced strawberries.
Per Serving: Calories 177.6 Carbohydrates 25.5g; Protein 5 g; Fat 8.9g; Sodium 286.5mg; Fiber 2.5g

Tropical Lemon Whipped Cream Pie

Prep time: 5 minutes | Cook Time: 17 minutes | Serves: 2

Ingredients:

3 tablespoons sweetened condensed milk
1 teaspoon egg yolk
2 teaspoons lemon juice
Whipped cream, for serving
2 ½ tablespoons desiccated coconut
⅛ teaspoon lemon rind, grated
1 packet sugar cookie dough

Preparation:

1. Butter the Easy-Bake Oven baking pan. 2. Take out the sugar cookie dough. Press it into the pan and up the sides. 3. Bake in the Easy-Bake Oven for 5 minutes. 4. While it's baking, mix together the egg yolk, lemon juice, condensed milk, 2 tablespoons coconut, and grated lemon rind. 5. Remove the pan from the oven. Pour the lemon mixture onto the crust. 6. Bake in the Easy-Bake Oven for 12 minutes. Allow the pie to cool completely in the pan.
Serving Suggestion: Add whipped cream on top with the remaining coconut, then serve.
Variation Tip: Sprinkle chopped nuts for extra flavor.
Per Serving: Calories 155.5; Carbohydrates 24.8g; Protein 3g; Fat 5.4g; Sodium 193.7mg; Fiber 1g

Cherry Pie

Prep time: 5 minutes | Cook Time: 30 minutes | Serves: 2

Ingredients:

⅓ cup pie crust mix
4 teaspoons water
6 teaspoon cherry pie filling

Preparation:

1. In a small bowl, combine the pie crust mix and water with a fork. Stir the mixture gently to form a ball. 2. Divide the dough in half, forming 2 small balls. 3. On a floured board, roll out one ball slightly larger than the Easy-Bake Oven baking pan. Fit it into the greased pan. 4. Fill with the pie filling. 5. Roll out the second ball of dough and place it on top. Seal the edges with a fork. 6. Bake in the Easy-Bake Oven for 25 to 30 minutes.
Serving Suggestion: Serve with whipped cream on top.
Variation Tip: Add some candied cherries on top before serving.
Per Serving: Calories 143.8; Carbohydrates 20.3; Protein 2.6g; Fat 5.8g; Sodium 196.4mg; Fiber 0.5g

Blueberry Pie

Prep time: 5 minutes | Cook Time: 30 minutes | Serves: 2

Ingredients:

⅓ cup pie crust mix
4 teaspoons water
6 teaspoons blueberry pie filling

Preparation:

1. In a small bowl, combine the pie crust mix and water with a fork. Stir the mixture gently to form a ball. 2. Divide the dough in half, forming 2 small balls. 3. On a floured board, roll out one ball slightly larger than the Easy-Bake Oven baking pan. Fit it into the greased pan. 4. Fill with the pie filling. 5. Roll out the second ball of dough and place it on top. Seal the edges with a fork. 6. Bake in the Easy-Bake Oven for 25 to 30 minutes.

Serving Suggestion: Serve with whipped cream on top.

Variation Tip: Add some fresh blueberries before serving.

Per Serving: Calories 89.5; Carbohydrates 4.1g; Protein 0.2g; Fat 8.3g; Sodium 50.4mg; Fiber 0.2g

Caramel Apple Tart

Prep time: 5 minutes | Cook Time: 12 minutes | Serves: 2

Ingredients:

1 packet sugar cookie dough
3 teaspoons sweetened condensed milk
1 teaspoon egg yolk
2 teaspoons apple juice
1 teaspoon caramel topping
¼ apple, cut into small slices, for serving
Whipped cream, for serving

Preparation:

1. Take out the cookie dough and press it into a greased Easy-Bake Oven baking pan and up its sides. 2. Bake in the Easy-Bake Oven for 5 minutes. 3. Meanwhile, mix the egg yolk, apple juice, and condensed milk in a bowl. 4. Pour the mixture onto the crust. 5. Bake in the Easy-Bake Oven for 12 minutes. 6. Cool the completely in the pan. 7. Run a knife around the edge of the tart, then turn it over gently. Do NOT touch the apple center. 8. Apply the caramel topping and whipped cream around the outside of the tart and garnish it with apple slices on top.

Serving Suggestion: Serve with ice cream.

Variation Tip: You can add some chopped nuts for flavor.

Per Serving: Calories 151; Carbohydrates 19.46g; Protein 1.85g; Fat 7.54g; Sodium 95mg; Fiber 0.4g

Fruit Tart

Prep time: 5 minutes | Cook Time: 5-8 minutes | Serves: 2

Ingredients:

7 teaspoons shortening
7 teaspoons sugar
Pinch of salt
¼ cup flour
⅛ teaspoon baking powder
⅛ teaspoon vanilla extract

For the topping:

4 strawberries, sliced
6 blueberries
Whipped cream
Individual size container vanilla pudding

Preparation:

1. Cream together the butter, sugar, and salt in a bowl. 2. Add the flour, baking powder, and vanilla. Mix until a ball of dough forms. 3. Sprinkle 1 teaspoon of flour on the countertop. Roll the tart dough out, then use a knife to cut it into 1-inch circles. 4. Place the tarts on a greased Easy-Bake Oven baking pan. You may need to cook in batches. 5. Bake for 5 minutes in the Easy-Bake Oven. Wait for the tarts to cool, then remove them from the oven. 6. Spread some vanilla pudding on top of each tart, add some fruit, and top with whipped cream.

Serving Suggestion: Serve with a scoop of vanilla ice cream.

Variation Tip: You can use any fruit you like.

Per Serving: Calories 120; Carbohydrates 16g; Protein 1g; Fat 6g; Sodium 60mg; Fiber 2g

Apple Pie

Prep time: 5 minutes | Cook Time: 30 minutes | Serves: 2

Ingredients:

⅓ cup pie crust mix
4 teaspoons water
6 teaspoon apple pie filling

Preparation:

1. In a small bowl, combine the pie crust mix and water with a fork. Stir the mixture gently to form a ball. 2. Divide the dough in half, forming 2 small balls. 3. On a floured board, roll out one ball slightly larger than the Easy-Bake Oven baking pan. Fit it into the greased pan. 4. Fill with the pie filling. 5. Roll out the second ball of dough and place it on top. Seal the edges with a fork. 6. Bake in the Easy-Bake Oven for 25 to 30 minutes.

Serving Suggestion: Serve with whipped cream on top.

Variation Tip: Add some ground cinnamon for flavor.

Per Serving: Calories 251.8; Carbohydrates 33.7g; Protein 2.6g; Fat 12.3g; Sodium 185.7mg; Fiber 0.6g

Chapter 8 Snacks

Marshmallow Mud

Prep time: 10 minutes | Cook Time: 5 minutes | Serves: 2

Ingredients:

¼ cup rice cereal
5 small marshmallows
2 tablespoons chocolate chips

Preparation:

1. Put the cereal in the prepared baking pan. 2. Put the chocolate chips over the cereal. 3. Add the marshmallows. 4. Press the mixture down a bit 5. Put the pan in the oven and bake for 5 minutes. 6. Enjoy!
Serving Suggestion: Serve with a drizzle of chocolate syrup on top.
Variation Tip: You can add some chopped nuts.
Per Serving: Calories 138; Fat 4g |Sodium 36mg; Carbs 25.2g; Fiber 0.5g; Sugar 16g; Protein 1.2g

Cinnamon Crisp

Prep time: 10 minutes | Cook Time: 20 minutes | Serves: 2

Ingredients:

1 cup flour
½ teaspoon salt
6 teaspoons shortening
2 tablespoons ice water
Pinch of cinnamon
Pinch of sugar

Preparation:

1. Combine the flour and shortening in a bowl. 2. Add the water and stir to make a dough. 3. Roll the dough out on a lightly floured flat surface. 4. Sprinkle the top of the dough with the cinnamon, salt, and sugar. 5. Cut into shapes. Triangles work well. 6. Put the shapes onto the prepared baking pan. 7. Bake in the oven until the crisp turns brown, about 20 minutes.
Serving Suggestion: Serve with jelly.
Variation Tip: None—this recipe is perfect as it is!
Per Serving: Calories 342; Fat 13.4g; Sodium 583mg; Carbs 0g; Fiber 1.8g; Sugar 0.4g; Protein 6.5g

Rice Krispies Treats

Prep time: 40 minutes | Cook Time: 5 minutes | Serves: 2

Ingredients:

2 teaspoons butter
4 teaspoons marshmallow cream
4 tablespoons Rice Krispies cereal

Preparation:

1. Combine the marshmallow cream and butter in a bowl. Place them in the prepared baking pan. 2. Melt them in the oven for 5 minutes. 3. Mix the cereal with the marshmallow mixture. 4. Form the mixture into cookie shapes. Place the shapes on a plate and put them in the refrigerator until they become solid (about 30 minutes). 5. Serve!

Serving Suggestion: Serve with a drizzle of chocolate syrup on top.

Variation Tip: Use margarine instead of butter.

Per Serving: Calories 214; Fat 6g; Sodium 88mg; Carbs 38g; Fiber 0g; Sugar 20g; Protein 1g

Popcorn Balls

Prep time: 10 minutes | Cook Time: 2 minutes | Serves: 1

Ingredients:

½ cup caramel syrup, candy, or topping
½ cup popped popcorn, unsalted

Preparation:

1. Put the caramel in the prepared baking pan and melt it in the oven for 2 minutes. 2. Pour the caramel over the popcorn. 3. Using your hands, form small balls from the mixture. Place on a parchment paper-lined plate. 4. Chill the popcorn balls before serving.

Serving Suggestion: Serve with salted nuts.

Variation Tip: None, this recipe is delicious as it is!

Per Serving: Calories 116; Fat 0.1g; Sodium 18mg; Carbs 27.7g; Fiber 0.3g; Sugar 25g; Protein 0.3g

Cheese Balls

Prep time: 12 minutes | Cook Time: 15 minutes | Serves: 2

Ingredients:

2 tablespoons margarine
1 tablespoon self-rising flour
1⁄3 cup cheese, grated
¼ cup Rice Krispies

Preparation:

1. Mix all the ingredients in a bowl. Combine well. 2. Shape small balls from the mixture with your hands. 3. Place the balls on the prepared baking pan. 4. Bake for 15 minutes.

Serving Suggestion: Serve with your choice of dip.

Variation Tip: Use your favorite type of cheese.

Per Serving: Calories 840; Fat 14g; Sodium 1843mg; Carbs 93.1g; Fiber 0.4g; Sugar 44g; Protein 25g

Honey Bunches Snack

Prep time: 15 minutes | Cook Time: 5 minutes | Serves: 2

Ingredients:

¼ cup Honey Bunches of Oats cereal
¼ cup Life cereal
1 tablespoon honey
1 tablespoon peanuts, divided

Preparation:

1. Mix the cereals together. Pour honey over the top and mix. 2. Spoon half of the mixture into the baking pan (you'll bake the other half next). Sprinkle with ½ tablespoon of peanuts. 3. Bake in the Easy-Bake Oven for 5 minutes or until done. 4. Allow it to cool completely. Repeat for the remaining mixture.

Serving Suggestion: Serve with chocolate buttercream or frosting on top.

Variation Tip: You can use other brand cereals.

Per Serving: Calories 205; Carbohydrates 29g; Protein 4g; Fat 7.7g; Sodium 150mg; Fiber 1g; Sugars 16g

Nachos 'N Cheese

Prep time: 5 minutes | Cook Time: 9 minutes | Serves: 2

Ingredients:

4 teaspoons processed cheese spread, soft
1 teaspoon water
Nacho chips

Preparation:

1. Mix the cheese and water in an Easy-Bake Oven-safe cup and cover. 2. Place it in the Easy-Bake Oven until the mixture softens. 3. Pour the mixture over nacho chips or use it as a dip.
Serving Suggestion: Sprinkle some grated cheese and chopped cilantro on top.
Variation Tip: Add fresh salsa, sour cream, and guacamole.
Per Serving: Calories 270; Carbohydrates 38g; Protein 3g; Fat 12g; Sodium 250mg; Fiber 1g

Chocolate Tostadas

Prep time: 5 minutes | Cook Time: 15 minutes | Serves: 2

Ingredients:

¼ cup plus 1 tablespoon heavy cream
1 teaspoon sugar
1-ounce chocolate
2 tablespoons butter
1 flour tortilla
Ground cinnamon, for sprinkling
Granulated sugar, for sprinkling

Preparation:

1. Combine the ¼ cup of heavy cream with the teaspoon of sugar. Whip until soft peaks form, taking care not to over-whip. Keep chilled until ready to serve. 2. Place the chocolate in an Easy-Bake Oven baking pan. Add the remaining 1 tablespoon of heavy cream, and then bake in the Easy-Bake Oven for 5 minutes. 3. Remove the pan from the oven. Stir to combine. Transfer the mixture to a bowl. 4. Wash and dry the baking pan. 5. Melt the butter in the microwave. 6. Place the Easy-Bake Oven baking pan upside down, directly on top of the tortilla, and cut around the perimeter of the pan to form a smaller tortilla the exact size and shape of the pan. Repeat, so you have two tortillas. 7. Using a pastry brush or paper towel, butter the inside of the Easy-Bake Oven pan. 8. Press a tortilla into the pan, then brush the top of the tortilla entirely with the melted butter. Sprinkle the cinnamon and sugar over the tortilla, as you would for cinnamon toast. 9. Bake in the Easy-Bake Oven for 10 minutes, until crispy and golden. 10. Remove from the oven, and serve.
Serving Suggestion: Serve topped with the chocolate sauce and whipped cream you made earlier.
Variation Tip: Add some vanilla extract for taste.
Per Serving: Calories 181.5; Carbohydrates 23.4g; Protein 5.1g; Fat 3g; Sodium 266 mg; Fiber 0g

Cinnamon Raisin Pockets

Prep time: 5 minutes | Cook Time: 10 minutes | Serves: 2

Ingredients:

¼ of 8-ounce can crescent rolls
2 teaspoons butter, melted
2 tablespoons raisins
Ground cinnamon, to taste
Sugar, to taste

For the sugar frosting:
2 teaspoons water
2 drops vanilla extract
¼ cup powdered sugar

Preparation:

1. Divide the crescent roll dough in half. Shape the dough into 2 rectangles. 2. Brush one rectangle with butter. Sprinkle with cinnamon and sugar. Top with the raisins. 3. Place the second dough rectangle on top. 4. Cut it into 8 squares. Pinch the sides of the squares to seal. 5. Place the squares into an ungreased Easy-Bake Oven baking pan. You may need to bake in batches. 6. Bake in the Easy-Bake Oven until golden brown, about 10 minutes. 7. Meanwhile, make the sugar frosting: Combine the water, vanilla, and powdered sugar in a bowl. Mix until smooth. 8. When the pockets are done, drizzle with the frosting and let them cool.

Serving Suggestion: Serve with a dusting of powdered sugar.
Variation Tip: Add some grated apple for extra flavor.
Per Serving: Calories 233; Carbohydrates 34g; Protein 2g; Fat 9g; Sodium 153mg; Fiber 1g

Chocolate Covered Pretzels

Prep time: 5 minutes | Cook Time: 10 minutes | Serves: 2

Ingredients:

½ cup mini chocolate chips
1 teaspoon shortening
10 long pretzel logs
Colored sugar

Preparation:

1. Put the mini chocolate chips and shortening in an Easy-Bake Oven-safe bowl. Heat in the Easy-Bake Oven until the mixture is hot and pourable. 2. Hold a pretzel log over a plate. Spoon the chocolate mixture over both ends of the log. Place the log on a sheet of wax paper. 3. Sprinkle with the colored sugar. 4. Repeat for the remaining logs. 5. Let stand about 1 hour or until the melted mixture firms onto the pretzel logs.

Serving Suggestion: Serve as a snack with milk.
Variation Tip: You can also use colored sprinkles.
Per Serving: Calories 270; Carbohydrates 38g; Protein 3g; Fat 12g; Sodium 250mg; Fiber 1g

Hot Dog Cheese Crackers

Prep time: 5 minutes | Cook Time: 10 minutes | Serves: 4

Ingredients:

8 crackers
2 slices American cheese, cut into 4 squares
1 hot dog, cut into 8 slices

Preparation:

1. Place one square of cheese onto each cracker. Top with a slice of hot dog. 2. Place the crackers on an ungreased Easy-Bake Oven baking pan. 3. Bake in the Easy-Bake Oven until the cheese melts.

Serving Suggestion: Serve hot.

Variation Tip: You can also make this snack with cooked meatballs.

Per Serving: Calories 201.5; Carbohydrates 25g; Protein 2.8g; Fat 10.2g; Sodium 62.7mg; Fiber 0.4g

Chocolate Balls

Prep time: 5 minutes | Cook Time: 10 minutes | Serves: 2

Ingredients:

2 chocolate cookies
1 tablespoon coconut, shredded
1 tablespoon sweetened condensed milk
Chocolate sprinkles

Preparation:

1. Crush the cookies finely in a bowl. 2. Add the coconut and cocoa and mix well. Stir in the condensed milk. 3. Form the mixture into balls and then roll the balls in the chocolate sprinkles. 4. Chill in the refrigerator until firm.

Serving Suggestion: Serve with a milkshake.

Variation Tip: You can add chopped nuts for crunch.

Per Serving: Calories 407.8; Carbohydrates 49.3g; Protein 4.3g; Fat 11.3g; Sodium 484.2mg; Fiber 0.5g

Caramel Corn

Prep time: 2 minutes | Cook Time: 9 minutes | Serves: 2

Ingredients:

2 teaspoons caramel topping

½ cup unsalted popped popcorn

Preparation:

1. Place the caramel topping in an Easy-Bake Oven-safe cup. 2. Put the cup on the Easy-Bake Oven pan and warm in the Easy-Bake Oven until it's pourable. 3. Put the popcorn in a bowl. Drizzle the warm mixture over the popcorn and stir.

Serving Suggestion: Serve warm and enjoy.

Variation Tip: Use a little sea salt to enhance the flavor.

Per Serving: Calories 39.55; Carbohydrates 4.12g; Protein 0.6g; Fat 2.31g; Sodium 114.32mg; Fiber 0.4g

Bean Dip Nachos

Prep time: 5 minutes | Cook Time: 10 minutes | Serves: 1

Ingredients:

½ cup round tortilla chips

1 teaspoon bean dip

1 teaspoon cheese, grated

Preparation:

1. Place the tortilla chips on an ungreased Easy-Bake Oven baking pan. 2. Top with about 1 teaspoon of bean dip and 1 teaspoon of grated cheese. 3. Bake in the Easy-Bake Oven until the cheese is melted.

Serving Suggestion: Serve with extra grated cheese, sour cream, guacamole, and salsa.

Variation Tip: Use any kind of cheese you prefer.

Per Serving: Calories 98; Carbohydrates 7.1g; Protein 1.3g; Fat 6.5g; Sodium 154.6mg; Fiber 0g

Bacon Roll-Ups

Prep time: 5 minutes | Cook Time: 15 minutes | Serves: 2

Ingredients:

⅛ cup sour cream
⅛ teaspoon onion salt
1 tablespoon bacon bits
¼ of 8-ounce package crescent rolls

Preparation:

1. Carefully separate out the crescent rolls. 2. Mix the sour cream, onion salt, and bacon in a bowl. 3. Spread the mixture onto the rolls. 4. Cut each roll into four and roll them up. 5. Place the rolls on the Easy-Bake Oven baking pan. You'll need to cook in batches. 6. Bake in the Easy-Bake Oven for 12 to 15 minutes.

Serving Suggestion: Serve warm with cheese sauce.

Variation Tip: Use chopped dill for garnish.

Per Serving: Calories 577; Carbohydrates 73g; Protein 6.6g; Fat 30g; Sodium 415mg; Fiber 1.6g

Prep time: 5 minutes | Cook Time: 25 minutes | Serves: 2

Ingredients:

2 tablespoons apple pie filling
1 8-inch flour tortilla
⅛ teaspoon ground cinnamon

For the sauce:

3 teaspoons margarine
1 tablespoon white sugar
1 tablespoon packed brown sugar
1 tablespoon water

Preparation:

1. Cut the tortilla to fit into the Easy-Bake Oven baking pan. (Turn the pan upside down, place it on the tortilla, and cut around the edge.) 2. Spoon the apple pie evenly onto the tortilla. Sprinkle with the cinnamon. 3. Roll up the tortilla and it into the lightly greased baking pan. 4. Bake in the Easy-Bake Oven for 5 minutes. 5. Meanwhile, combine the margarine, sugars, and water in a saucepan. Melt the mixture on medium heat. 6. Pour the sauce evenly over the tortilla; sprinkle with extra cinnamon on top if desired. Bake in the Easy-Bake Oven for 20 minutes.

Serving Suggestion: Serve with chocolate sauce.

Variation Tip: None; this recipe is delicious as it is!

Per Serving: Calories 233; Carbohydrates 34g; Protein 2g; Fat 9g; Sodium 153mg; Fiber 1g

Butter Cheese Twists

Prep time: 15 minutes | Cook Time: 15 minutes | Serves: 12

Ingredients:

Anti-sticking baking spray
3 teaspoons butter, melted
¾ cup cheese, grated
12-ounce can refrigerator crescent rolls
Garlic salt, to taste

Preparation:

1. Plug in the easy bake oven, preheating it for 15 minutes. 2. Spritz baking spray on the baking pan, followed by dusting with flour. 3. Split the dough into two portions and flatten them into rectangular shapes. 4. Seal any perforations by pressing them together. 5. Next, brush butter on the surface of first rectangle and then dash it with garlic salt and cheese. 6. Position the second dough rectangle on top of the first one at this point.7. Slice the dough into strips that are approximately ½ inch wide. 8. Twist each strip five times, and then firmly pinch the ends together to seal them. 9. Lay out twisted dough strips onto the baking pan about 1½-inch apart. 10. Bake in the preheated oven for 15 minutes. 11. After cooking time is finished, with pan pusher, shove the baking pan into the "Cooling Chamber". 12. Give it about five minutes to cool down. 13. Carefully turn the cheese twists onto a platter to serve and enjoy.

Per Serving: Calories 100; Fat 6.2g; Sodium 182mg; Carbs 7.7g; Fiber 0g; Sugar 1.4g; Protein 2.6g

Cheesy Biscuits

Prep time: 15 minutes | Cook Time: 10 minutes | Serves: 6

Ingredients:

¼ cup Bisquick, homemade
Anti-sticking baking spray
4 teaspoons milk
⅛ teaspoon garlic
2 tablespoons cheddar cheese, shredded
¼ teaspoon parsley
1 tablespoon butter
1 tablespoon Parmesan cheese

Preparation:

1. Plug in the easy bake oven, preheating it for 15 minutes. 2. Spritz baking spray on the baking pan, followed by dusting with flour. 3. Put milk and homemade Bisquick into medium-sized bowl and whisk to incorporate. 4. Fold in the cheddar and parmesan cheese. 5. Lay out the mixture onto the baking pan about 1½-inch apart. Mix up the garlic, parsley and butter in a small bowl and pou over the batter in the pan. 6. Bake in the preheated oven for 10 minutes. 7. After cooking time is finished, shove the baking pan into the "Cooling Chamber". 8. Give it about five minutes to cool down. 9. Cook the remnant cookies in the same way. 10. Serve and enjoy.

Per Serving: Calories 52; Fat 3.8g; Sodium 103mg; Carbs 3.5g; Fiber 0g; Sugar 0.3g; Protein 1.5g

Cheese Hot Dog Crackers

Prep time: 15 minutes | Cook Time: 8 minutes | Serves: 8

Ingredients:

2 squares American cheese, sliced into 4 squares
1 hot dog, cut into 8 slices
8 Ritz Crackers

Preparation:

1. Plug in the easy bake oven, preheating it for 15 minutes. 2. Position one square of cheese on each cracker, and then place a slice of hot dog on top. 3. Lay out crackers onto the baking pan. 4. Bake in the preheated oven for 8 minutes. 5. After cooking time is finished, with pan pusher, shove the baking pan into the "Cooling Chamber". 6. Give it about five minutes to cool down. 7. Carefully turn the crackers onto a platter to serve and enjoy.

Per Serving: Calories 166; Fat 9.2g; Sodium 368mg; Carbs 16.3g; Fiber 0.6g; Sugar 2.7g; Protein 3.7g

Rice Krispies Cheese Balls

Prep time: 15 minutes | Cook Time: 15 minutes | Serves: 6

Ingredients:

Anti-sticking baking spray
1 tablespoon self-rising flour
¼ cup rice krispies
2 tablespoons margarine
¼ cup mozzarella cheese, grated

Preparation:

1. Plug in the easy bake oven, preheating it for 15 minutes. 2. Spritz baking spray on the baking pan, followed by dusting with flour. 3. Merge all the ingredients into medium-sized bowl and roll into balls. 4. Lay out the cheese balls onto the baking pan about 1½-inch apart. 5. Bake in the preheated oven for 15 minutes. 6. After cooking time is finished, with pan pusher, shove the baking pan into the "Cooling Chamber". 7. Give it about five minutes to cool down. 8. Carefully turn the cheese balls onto a platter to serve and enjoy.

Per Serving: Calories 48; Fat 4.1g; Sodium 57mg; Carbs 2.3g; Fiber 0.1g; Sugar 0g; Protein 0.6g

Ham & Cheese Bagels

Prep time: 15 minutes | Cook Time: 15 minutes | Serves: 2

Ingredients:

1 slice deli ham
Anti-sticking baking spray
1 bagel, halved
4 tablespoons cheddar cheese

Preparation:

1. Plug in the easy bake oven, preheating it for 15 minutes. 2. Spritz baking spray on the baking pan, followed by dusting with flour. 3. Position a slice of ham onto a toasted bagel half. 4. In each of the warming cups of Easy-Bake Oven, divide the cheese. 5. Warm the cheese in a small microwave-safe bowl. 6. Trickle the warm cheese over the ham slice on the bagel. 7. Top the sandwich with the other toasted bagel half and assemble it. 8. Lay out sandwiches onto the baking pan. 9. Bake in the preheated oven for15 minutes. 10. After cooking time is finished, with pan pusher, shove the baking pan into the "Cooling Chamber". 11. Give it about five minutes to cool down. 12. Carefully turn the bagels onto a platter to serve and enjoy.

Per Serving: Calories 142; Fat 5.2g; Sodium 488mg; Carbs 16g; Fiber 0.8g; Sugar 2.5g; Protein 7.8g

Cheese Bird's Nest Breakfast Cups

Prep time: 10 minutes | Cook Time: 5 minutes | Serves: 6

Ingredients:

Anti-sticking baking spray
1 bag chow mein noodles
1 container red grapes
2 tablespoons honey
2 tablespoons jack cheese, grated

Preparation:

1. Plug in the easy bake oven, preheating it for 15 minutes. 2. Fill the baking pan with cheese. 3. Bake in the preheated oven for 5 minutes. 4. Place the chow mein noodles in a small bowl. 5. After cooking time is finished, drizzle melted cheese over the chow mein noodles and gently mix them together. 6. Quickly shape nests on waxed paper using approximately 2 tablespoons of the mixture for each nest. 7. Make sure to work swiftly so the cheese doesn't have time to harden. 8. Place a few small dots of honey inside each nest to assist in adhering the red grapes. 9. Serve immediately.

Per Serving: Calories 80; Fat 3.1g; Sodium 50mg; Carbs 12.5g; Fiber 0.5g; Sugar 7.8g; Protein 1.3g

Basic Cornbread

Prep time: 15 minutes | Cook Time: 15 minutes | Serves: 6

Ingredients:

2 teaspoons butter
2 tablespoons milk
Anti-sticking baking spray
1 tablespoon sugar
½ teaspoon baking soda
¼ cup flour, all-purpose
¼ teaspoon vanilla extract
1 tablespoon cornmeal

Preparation:

1. Plug in the easy bake oven, preheating it for 15 minutes. 2. Begin by dividing the dry and wet ingredients into separate bowls. 3. Merge both sets of ingredients in their respective bowls, then gradually merge the dry and wet ingredients. 4. While adding wet ingredients, continue to mix the mixture thoroughly. 5. Grease the baking pan with the baking spray. Lay out the mixture onto the baking pan about 1½-inch apart. 6. Bake in the preheated oven for 15 minutes. 7. After cooking time is finished, shift the baking pan on a countertop to cool down for approximately five minutes. 8. Carefully turn the cornbread onto a platter to serve and enjoy.

Per Serving: Calories 45; Fat 1.5g; Sodium 166mg; Carbs 7.2g; Fiber 0.2g; Sugar 2.3g; Protein 0.8g

Cheese Bean Dip Nachos

Prep time: 15 minutes | Cook Time: 10 minutes | Serves: 1

Ingredients:

1 teaspoon cheese, grated
Tortilla chips, round
1 teaspoon bean dip

Preparation:

1. Plug in the easy bake oven, preheating it for 15 minutes. 2. Put the tortilla chips on the baking pan. 3. Add bean dip and grated cheese on top. 4. Bake in the preheated oven for 10 minutes. 5. Cook the remnant cookies in the same way. 6. Carefully turn the nachos onto a platter to serve.

Per Serving: Calories 68; Fat 1.6g; Sodium 57mg; Carbs 11.6g; Fiber 1.8g; Sugar 0.2g; Protein 2.3g

Caramel Popcorn

Prep time: 15 minutes | Cook Time: 8 minutes | Serves: 2

Ingredients:

½ cup popcorn, unsalted
2 teaspoons caramel topping

Preparation:

1. Plug in the easy bake oven, preheating it for 15 minutes. 2. Spoon caramel topping in the baking pan. 3. Bake in the preheated oven for 8 minutes. 4. After cooking time is finished, trickle the warm mixture over popcorn and then stir it in thoroughly to serve.
Per Serving: Calories 25; Fat 0.1g; Sodium 24mg; Carbs 6.1g; Fiber 0.4g; Sugar 0g; Protein 0.4g

English Muffin Breakfast Pizza

Prep time: 15 minutes | Cook Time: 20 minutes | Serves: 2

Ingredients:

Anti-sticking baking spray
1 tablespoon spaghetti sauce, ready made
2 teaspoons mozzarella cheese, shredded
1 teaspoon mushrooms, sliced
1 English muffin, split
2 teaspoons pepperoni slices

Preparation:

1. Plug in the easy bake oven, preheating it for 15 minutes. 2. Spritz baking spray on the baking pan, followed by dusting with flour. 3. Position one half of an English muffin in the pan. 4. Add spaghetti sauce to each English muffin half. 5. Add mushrooms and pepperoni slices. 6. Sprinkle the shredded cheese on top of each muffin half. 7. Bake in the preheated oven for 20 minutes. 8. After cooking time is finished, with pan pusher, shove the baking pan into the "Cooling Chamber". 9. Give it about five minutes to cool down. 10. Carefully turn the cookies onto a platter to serve and enjoy.
Per Serving: Calories 106; Fat 2.7g; Sodium 636mg; Carbs 15.9g; Fiber 1.2g; Sugar 1g; Protein 4.5g

Pepperoni Pizza

Prep time: 15 minutes | Cook Time: 20 minutes | Serves: 2

Ingredients:

2 tablespoons flour, all-purpose
⅛ teaspoon baking powder
Anti-sticking baking spray
1 teaspoon butter, softened
1 tablespoon pizza sauce
8 mini pepperoni slices
1 dash salt
2¼ teaspoons milk
1½ tablespoon shredded mozzarella cheese

Preparation:

1. Plug in the easy bake oven, preheating it for 15 minutes. 2. In a bowl, merge the flour with remaining ingredients except the milk until coarse. 3. While continuously stirring, gradually incorporate the milk into the mixture until it forms a dough. 4. Using the dough, form a ball and then position it in the center of the greased baking pan. 5. Press the pizza dough out to cover the pan and extend it halfway up the sides. 6. Evenly spread sauce over pizza dough. 7. Sprinkle the shredded cheese on top and position the pepperoni slices evenly over cheese. 8. Bake in the preheated oven for 20 minutes. 9. After cooking time is finished, with pan pusher, shove the baking pan into the "Cooling Chamber". 10. Give it about five minutes to cool down. 11. Carefully turn the pizza onto a platter and serve to enjoy.

Per Serving: Calories 221; Fat 15.6g; Sodium 614mg; Carbs 8g; Fiber 0.4g; Sugar 0.5g; Protein 12.1g

Mozzarella Quesadillas

Prep time: 20 minutes | Cook Time: 6 minutes | Serves: 3

Ingredients:

1 tortilla
Anti-sticking baking spray
½ cup mozzarella cheese, shredded

Preparation:

1. Plug in the easy bake oven, preheating it for 10 minutes. 2. Spritz baking spray on the baking pan, followed by dusting with flour. 3. Slice a small flour tortilla into wedges that are small enough to fit the pan. 4. Create a cheese sandwich by placing shredded cheese between two of these tortilla wedges. 5. Lay tortilla wedges onto the baking pan. 6. Bake in the preheated oven for 6 minutes. 7. After cooking time is finished, carefully turn the quesadillas onto a platter to serve and enjoy.

Per Serving: Calories 31; Fat 1.1g; Sodium 32mg; Carbs 3.7g; Fiber 0.5g; Sugar 0.1g; Protein 1.8g

Conclusion

There's not much that you can't cook in an Easy-Bake Oven. After all, it works just like a conventional oven, only it's smaller! There are so many yummy yet straightforward recipes for kids to create using this device. As long as the child is over eight years of age and has adult supervision, they can use the Easy-Bake Oven to cook snacks, mains, biscuits, cakes, and more.

For all eager little bakers out there, the Easy-Bake Oven is possibly the most appreciated gift of all. So, don't hesitate; get the small chef in your life an Easy-Bake Oven and help them create delicious little treats. Happy baking!

Appendix Recipes Index

Made in United States
Troutdale, OR
11/25/2024

25237978R00065